# International Negotiations: Theory and Practice

Jang Hee Yoo Series on International Studies
is published with financial support from
the Specialization Committee on International Studies,
Ewha Womans University

# International Negotiations: Theory and Practice

*By*
BYUNG-IL CHOI & BRENDAN M. HOWE

**Ewha Womans University Press**

*International Negotiations: Theory and Practice*
By BYUNG-IL CHOI & BRENDAN M. HOWE



First published 30 January, 2007
Published by Ewha Womans University Press
11-1 Daehyun-dong, Seodaemun-gu, Seoul, Korea 120-750
Tel. (82-2)3277-3164, 362-6076
Fax. (82-2)312-4312
E-mail: press@ewha.ac.kr
Online Bookstore: http://www.ewhapress.com

price: 10,000won / U.S.$10.00

ISBN 978-89-7300-732-5 93300

# Foreword

This is the fifth volume in the Jang-Hee Yoo Series on International Studies developed by the Specialization Committee on International Studies of Ewha Womans University. We began this series with the goal of establishing the relatively new field named International Studies with two ideas in mind:

(1) The contemporary international environment is rapidly changing with the whole world becoming accessible. Our frame of reference on a daily basis, whether you live in a remote village or in a cosmopolitan metropolis, is no longer our community or nation, but the globe. Even in remote corners of the world we are amazed to learn that people, products and services of other nations find their way there as tourists, import products, via internet, CNN, and phones to name a few. International governmental as well as non-governmental organizations are increasingly playing an important role since people feel the need to be connected, to have conflicts resolved, and to mediate in international affairs. We felt it was critical to develop an interdisciplinary field of knowledge that would help us grapple with the complexities of this New World.

(2) In order to solve problems in this rapidly changing and globalized world an interdisciplinary tool box was needed. You cannot rely on knowledge and skills you gain from one field (discipline) to tackle the multi-faceted problems we have today. In fact, even in the aftermath of the 2004

> Tsunami that hit Southeast Asian nations we found that it was not simply a matter of getting rescue workers out to the Tsunami stricken areas. The relief efforts for even a natural disaster like the Tsunami required international organizations, insurance agents, medical crew, international lawyers and many others to be on the scene within days of the crisis. The world in which we live and the problems we face require an entirely different set of skills than those we needed just twenty years ago. We felt that International Studies should provide the necessary skills from multiple disciplines to solve the world's problems.

This book on international negotiations comes out of this context for wanting to "understand" and "solve" problems we face in this new world. In particular, the problems in the world increasingly compel us to find ways to solve problems in a peaceful manner. In an ever-more interdependent world it is vital that we learn how to understand our differences as we face people and societies of greater diversity with whom we probably would not have interacted fifty years ago. Thus, we need to learn how to communicate and understand across borders, cultures, disciplines and history without engaging in warfare and conflict. Furthermore, it is critically important in economic globalization that we learn how to negotiate well with our business partners, and to have winning outcomes for both (all) parties in bi-lateral and multi-lateral negotiations.

As South Korea is in the midst of several Free Trade Agreement Negotiations, including the KOR-US Negotiations, I hope our readers will find this as a useful book to help them guide through their tough negotiations, but also as a thoughtful book that will help them think about the complexities of this new world.

I am delighted that this book has finally come out during a time when negotiations at the national level are of paramount significance, and when there is no activity in the world that is not global. I would like to congratulate the two authors for an excellent volume, and to wish the field of International Studies to flourish in the years to come to help us better understand and cope with this globalized world.

Eun Mee Kim
Dean, Graduate School of International Studies,
Ewha Womans University

# Contents

# About the Authors

## Byung-il Choi

Byung-il Choi is a professor of international trade and negotiations, at the Graduate School of International Studies (GSIS), Ewha Womans University. He is also the Director of the Institute for International Trade and Cooperation at Ewha Womans University.

Prior to joining Ewha GSIS as a founding faculty member, Professor Choi was a trade negotiator representing the Korean government. He started his negotiating career at the Korea-US telecommunication talks (1990-1992), was the Korean chief negotiator for the historic WTO basic telecom negotiations (1994-1997), and played a key role in securing the agreement. He also worked for the Korea-EU negotiations, APEC, and was the Convener of the APEC telecom working group (1996-1997). Professor Choi advised both the South Korean government and the Indonesian government on telecommunication restructuring. His outstanding performance in the international arena led to him winning two medals of excellence from the Ministry of Information and Communications in 1991 and 1995.

Professor Choi has researched on international trade, corporate policy, political economy of development, and conflict resolution. His book, *the Success and Failure of Trade Negotiations of Korea* (2004), earned him the Korean Academy of Arts and Sciences Award, and his recent work, *Korea and International Conflicts: Case Studies, Volume 1* (2005), and *Volume 2* (2006) contain some landmark trade dispute cases including those involving the screen quota, Chinese garlic, and rice. In 2006, Professor Choi wrote *Against the All Odds: the Korea-US FTA, Framework for Advancement*, which was listed as one of the top 10 books of the year.

Professor Choi has served as the secretary general of the Korean Economic Association and the Korean International Economic Association. He serves the editorial board of *the Global Economic Review, the International Studies Review, and the International Area and Regional Studies*. He received a B.A. from Seoul National University with summa cum laude and a Ph.D. economics from Yale.

**Brendan M. Howe**

Brendan M. Howe is an international theorist from the West of England, trained at Oxford University (B.A. / M.A. Modern History); UKC (M.A. International Conflict Analysis); Trinity College Dublin (Ph.D. Political Science) and Georgetown University (International Law). He joined Ewha GSIS/DIS in 2001 and lectures primarily on international negotiations, security, organization and politics. He is also the Director of the International Studies Program (ISP) summer and winter intensive study courses.

In 2003 he was trained and certified as a Negotiation Workshop Facilitator at the Conflict Management Group, Cambridge, Massachusetts, and also completed a two month assignment as a POSCO Research Fellow in Politics, Governance and Security at the East-West Center in Hawaii. Previous posts include Visiting Professor of History and IR at Beijing Foreign Studies University (1993-1994) and International Relations Lecturer at Universiti Malaysia Sarawak (1995-1997).

He has published extensively on international security, intervention, and international norms. Current research interests include rationality, international societal constraints upon crisis decision-making and East Asian security regimes.

The authors gratefully acknowledge the help and advice of Devin Joshi and Bliss Park with early drafts of the manuscripts, Dean Eun Mee Kim of the Graduate School of International Studies at Ewha Womans University for her unflagging support and encouragement, and former Vice-President Jang-Hee Yoo of Ewha Womans University for his inspirational leadership in the field of International Studies.

# Chapter 1 Introduction

## 1.1 What do we mean by international negotiation?

Negotiations form the bed-rock of all human interactions whether social, political or economic. In almost all forms of interaction we encounter positions dissimilar from our own, and interests which may conflict with what we would ideally hope to take from any given situation. The resolution of conflicting interests or an attempt to reach a transaction that satisfies all parties to a greater or lesser extent for the creation of a greater collective good are facets of the process called negotiation.

This book emphasizes how rational and strategic underpinnings dictate the course of negotiations. Rational and game-theoretical modeling is used to give a greater understanding of these mechanisms, and to identify problems often associated with collective action of this kind. Throughout, although many of the analytical elements are applicable to all negotiating environments, emphasis is placed upon the international context.

In addition to these theoretical perspectives, throughout the book real world examples are used to illustrate some of the important concepts and the second half of the book is specifically dedicated to the practice of international negotiations. In particular, the close relationship between negotiation and conflict will be explored. In almost all negotiations conflicts of interest present obstacles that must be overcome.

At the same time, wherever there is conflict there is likely to be hope for a negotiated settlement, as much conflict is due to the *perception* of incompatible interests, and the tendency of all parties to take positions that neglect shared interests, 'demonizing' the other while 'sanctifying' their own actions and self-perception. Much of the methodology contained in this volume is specifically directed at correcting misperceptions, allowing for alternative interpretations of data, and facilitating communications aimed at reducing conflict.

This book is aimed at helping students develop:

- conceptual frameworks for analyzing conflicts;
- insight into styles of resolving conflicts;
- an understanding of problems prevalent in the international arena;
- a broader repertoire of negotiation strategies and skills; and
- a deeper understanding of how to work with conflict.

## 1.2 The Audience

This book is aimed to provide an introduction to the cornerstones of international negotiation for both the scholar and the practitioner. In many cases the reader is directed to further, more advanced, or more specific readings, but having read this book she will at least have a good underpinning before further exploration.

The authors have combined their theoretical and practical backgrounds in order to provide a more holistic approach to the field. In addition, coming from different academic disciplines themselves, they have attempted to make sure that this book remains relevant to all students and practitioners from all the subject areas that engage in the analysis or practice of international negotiations.

## 1.3 Related Disciplines

The relationship between international negotiation and other academic disciplines can be found in three areas: The theoretical underpinnings of understanding, analysis and application in international negotiation; the real world application of international negotiation theory in different fields of endeavor; and the evolving field of conflict analysis, management, and resolution.

Many of the game-theoretical elements of international negotiation originated in their application from the economic branches of the social sciences. However, as will be seen from a reading of this book, political and moral philosophers, psychologists, mathematicians and lawyers have all contributed to the evolution of the large body of work that is known as international negotiations theory.

Likewise, while, with globalization, those with an economic or trade background increasingly find themselves negotiating across boundaries, international negotiations have always been at the heart of international diplomacy, international law and international organizations.

Conflict *per se* is not necessarily or universally seen as a negative. Much human progress has come about as a result of dynamic conflict between individuals, groups, or between actors and their environment. Conflict in the form of challenges that need to be overcome has often formed the impetus for innovation, change, and evolution. However, the most extreme manifestations of the conflict phenomena have increasingly been seen as, on balance, harmful to the interests of those involved and detrimental to the collective production of common goods.

The most obvious form of detrimental conflict is warfare. Few would now agree with nineteenth century social Darwinists that war is actually good for mankind, and for the individual nations and their peoples involved. Not surprisingly then, the initial impetus for the understanding of the causes of conflict in order that its worst manifestations might be mitigated or even eliminated came from the 'high political' arenas of security studies and international organization.

The United Nations structure includes a number of mechanisms for the peaceful resolution of disputes, as did its forerunner, the League of Nations, which was set up with the express purpose of scientifically regulating conflict. Increasingly the focus has shifted from the management of existing (and perhaps intractable) conflicts, to the permanent resolution of conflict by identifying and modifying its underlying causes.

As the practitioners of various disciplines have also come to understand the detrimental effects of the worst manifestations of conflict in international negotiations in their own fields, so the ranks of conflict analysts and 'conflictologists' have been swelled with international lawyers and business school professors. Thus political scientists and practitioners like John Groom have been joined by members of the Harvard Negotiation Project led by Roger Fisher.

## 1.4 Chapter Overview

Chapter 2 follows on from this initial discussion on the nature of international negotiation. It pays particular attention to the examination of rational and strategic thinking that has come to form the basis of international negotiation theory. It introduces a number of the game-theoretical models and constructs that have been used in order to simplify and explain the negotiating process, and also in order to identify some of the underlying causes of conflict. It outlines ways in which some dilemmas can be overcome, but also acknowledges the shortcomings of several of these models when applied to the international arena.

Chapter 3 takes up where chapter 2 left off, expanding on the shortcomings of traditional rational modeling techniques when applied to the international negotiation environment, and also exploring more complex models that have been introduced in order to try to come to terms with these shortcomings. These more complex models in turn identify further rational and procedural problems, and additional causes of conflict. In particular, problems associated with the multilateral nature of international negotiations, the structure of international negotiations decision-making, the rationality and perceptions of individuals (particularly in cross-cultural negotiations) and crisis decision-making have demonstrated how far practice can at times seem to stray from theory. Where practicable, this chapter also introduces proposed mechanisms for dealing with these additional problems.

Chapter 4 examines further the problems associated with one particular characteristic of international negotiations – that in general they comprise two-level games. At one level there is the inter-governmental game, or the game played between the senior representatives of macro-level entities including multi-national corporations. At a subsidiary level, a separate but connected and influential game is played within the domestic jurisdiction of the state or corporation. Often the internal problems of the domestic games can impact greatly upon how the senior representatives play their hands in the larger, international game. Indeed, the range of negotiated agreements possible at the macro-level is often dependent upon what is acceptable to domestic constituencies, or forms part of their 'win-set.' This chapter also explores the roles of negotiators within this two-level framework, breaking them down into groupings of advocators, coordinators, and facilitators.

Chapter 5 continues this shift toward a more practical, real-world focus by looking in detail at the process of international negotiations. First, the general process of international negotiations is examined by breaking it down into its sequential components of agenda setting, the actual negotiations, the production of a final agreement, ratification of this agreement, and finally implementation. Second, this chapter explores dispute settlement mechanisms that have actually been employed in cases of international negotiation. Last, this chapter introduces the real world case study of the international Climate Change Convention in order that the reader may see for herself these procedures in practice.

Chapter 6 wraps up our introduction to the theory and practice of international negotiation by exploring the world of international negotiations strategy. First, it will introduce a basic framework including concepts such as BATNA (best alternative to negotiated agreement), win-sets, ZOPA (zone of potential agreement), value creation and claims, how to draft a final agreement, and the SMART (specific, measurable, achievable, realistic and time-frame) guideline. Second, it will explore the practical complexities of multilateral international negotiations in terms of process management, modality, and decision-rules. Finally, a number of case studies will put the theory to work.

# Chapter 2 International Negotiations Theory

## 2.1 Introduction

From a theoretical point of view, international negotiations concern the interaction between different entities, each of which presumably seeks to maximize its own interest. These entities can be states, companies, multi-national corporations, trade unions, international organizations, non-governmental organizations, or individuals representing any of these entities or acting on their own behalf. Each decision-maker makes choices after consideration of the expected outcome of their actions or inactions. Decision-makers take 'positions' (where they stand on a particular issue or what they want to happen in the world) in accordance with these considerations.

In taking a position, we are all, to a greater or lesser extent, guided by two sets of instructions informing us how to behave. The first set of instructions concerns the actor's perception of what is the 'right' position to take, and is closely related to what may be called 'normative' considerations. These rules can be legal, social, ethical, religious, or customary, and are to be not only in law courses and books, but also in ideas coming from politics, economics, business, trade, development, anthropology, sociology, and so on. The second set of instructions concerns what is the 'best' position to take in terms of benefiting the individual taking the position. This set of guidelines in particular is the basis of rational and strategic thinking and decision-making, and is what we will focus on in this chapter.

## 2.2 Rational Decision-Making

Rational decision-making follows a simple cost-benefit analysis. For each action I take I must consider how much benefit I will receive as a direct result of my action. And I also need to consider how much my action will cost me in terms of effort expended to achieve the desired result and any accompanying negative side-effects. At any one time there are likely to be a number of possible actions I can take with a number of possible outcomes resulting from my actions. Some desires are wanted more badly than others, or will be of more benefit, and obtaining different desires requires different input and expenditure of effort and resources.

It would therefore be 'rational' to construct a hierarchy of preferred outcomes (which would be the best result, then the next best, etc, all the way down to the least favored potential outcome – sometimes known as preference ordering) in conjunction with the costs associated with the various courses of action needed in order to achieve such results. As a result of such analysis, I may decide that it is not worth the trouble to go after my most preferred outcome or goal, but that I will instead settle for a slightly smaller amount of benefit but at a considerably reduced cost.

For example, as a high school student I knew what kind of grades I would require to get into my first choice university. As it turned out, by my final year, I was already pretty much guaranteed to get those grades. I could have spent the final year studying as hard as possible in order to get straight As, but this would have drastically affected my social life, and anyway, I reasoned, as long as I received good grades at a top university, nobody would ever care about the grades I received in high school. It may be that my decision-making was the result of an immature but rational process, and I might still suffer at some point from not achieving those straight As, but I certainly sacrificed far less of my social life, and still achieved a result that was satisfactory to me, if not optimal.

We will look at the concept of results being 'good enough' not to warrant further effort later in the next chapter. For now we will simply state that in international negotiation theory, we make the *a priori* assumption that decision-makers are 'rational' to the extent that they engage in 'goal-seeking behavior,' and that this involves the construction of a hierarchy of preferred outcomes and a cost-benefit analysis of both the actions required to attain these goals, and the degree of benefit imparted by the goals themselves.

Furthermore, it is not simply enough to rank our preferences; we also need to take into account the chances of good or bad outcomes resulting from our choices. Even if I want to get from A to B as fast as possible, it may not be rational for me to accelerate as fast as I can, as this will drastically increase my chances of crashing or being arrested. In addition, it is not enough to simply be a rational decision-maker. Decision-making does not take place in a vacuum. Operating environments enable and constrain the fulfillment of desires. An individual's own desires may well be incompatible or even mutually exclusive. This is even more likely when different individuals interact. The preferences and actions of other decision-makers form part of our operating environment.

In almost every case our decisions will impact upon other people and their decisions will impact upon us. The process we have so far addressed only looks at the thought process of an individual who is taking little or no account of how their actions will affect others, or how the actions and preferences of others could affect them. In the above personal example, I clearly did not give much consideration to the interests of my best friend whom I influenced to hang out with me, even though he did not have the same sort of guaranteed admittance to his first choice university as I had already secured. Likewise my decision-making process paid scant heed to the wishes of my parents who were worried about having a slacker for a son.

As I have already mentioned, my decision-making process may well have been immature, but worse than that, in international negotiation theory terms, by ignoring the impact of my actions upon others, I was not thinking or acting strategically. Social interaction forms the basis of bargaining, strategic decision-making and negotiation. When you take a position it is important to allow for a potential conflict of interests with others. This means making rational decisions based not only upon the likely additional costs of such conflict, but also the potential additional benefits caused by this interaction. Truly rational choices in international negotiation theory are based upon a combination of cost-benefit analysis, preference ordering through a utility-based hierarchy of outcomes, calculation of probabilities, awareness of the external operating environment and interaction with other decision-makers. The next section deals with the mechanics of such strategic actions.

## 2.3 Strategic Decision-Making

When, as part of our rational decision-making processes, we pause to think about the impact our actions will have upon others and incorporate the impact of the likely actions and reactions of others into our mental calculus, we are thinking strategically. One way that this process has been encapsulated in international negotiation theory is through the use of game theoretical models. Game theory has a background in mathematics and economics, but is now widely used to model many forms of social interaction where the players think and act strategically. Modeling helps to simplify our own decision-making by providing a likely cognitive map of our negotiating partners. In other words, assuming that the individuals we are dealing with are also acting rationally, it helps us predict what they are likely to do, and therefore build these actions and reactions into our own cost-benefit analysis.

To make it easier to simulate some of the complex mental acrobatics that all of us engage in when thinking strategically, social scientists have developed a number of game theoretical models. Although, as pointed out by Sidney Verba, 'no model and no theorist, no matter how committed to holistic principles, can encompass the totality of a situation' (1969, 25) rational modeling does help render narrative accounts amenable to testing, and separates the exogenous (external – i.e. strategic) from endogenous (internal) factors, and also specifies the causal links between them (Bates et al. 1998, 228). Through increased understanding of the thought processes we all engage in, we are better able to play the game of life to our advantage.

It is possible to play poker or tennis without understanding what skills can best be used when, and what strategy to use against a particular player under a particular set of circumstances, but you will probably lose. Strategic thinking starts with uncovering the basic skills employed in all negotiations or other forms of interaction, then it looks at how well endowed you are with the skills – what are your resources – then looks at how best to use them. There are lots of different strategies, and depending on circumstances any one of them may produce a better result in terms of pay-off than any of the others. The strategy that gives you the best pay-off is called your 'dominant strategy.' There are lots of different games that map the interactions of the dominant strategies of players under different conditions. The next section explores some of them.

## 2.4 Strategic Actions

### *2.4.1 Concentration of Forces*

Concentration of forces relates to the interaction between offensive and defensive strategies. Ideally, to win a game or a battle, your offensive capabilities should be concentrated at a weak point on the enemy's defensive line. However, this is easier said than done. Your opponent is likely to spot any offensive concentration, and concentrate their defensive resources to repel it. Therefore, sometimes it becomes strategically rational to attack with a weaker formation that is opposed by fewer resources than your strongest units. In sport this can mean passing the ball to another player rather than your most feared striker, because the latter may be man-marked, or even double-marked, while the former may be left with a virtually clear run at the goal. Alternatively, it might make sense to take the harder route to achieve your goal, rather than the easier, but also more easily anticipated alternative.

This means that your strongest offensive units may serve a tremendous strategic purpose by actually doing nothing more than drawing away opposing defensive reserves. This is the reasoning behind the feint, or the diversionary attack. At the very least, to try to ensure that the opposition does not concentrate their defensive forces in a manner that will thwart your attack, it makes sense to try to convey to them that the attack is coming elsewhere along their defensive line than is actually the case. Such strategic thinking and actions paid great dividends when the Allied forces invaded German-held France at Normandy during the Second World War rather than the closer and easier coast in the vicinity of Calais. Terrible as the cost of the battle was, it was but a fraction of what might have been expected had the Allied forces attacked the strongest German forces which were tied up around Calais.

Likewise, the value of an ally's military contribution can sometimes be measured in the numbers of opposition troops they tie down, whether or not they actually engage in the fighting. Strategic decision-making revolves around the concept of maximizing your offensive leverage while minimizing the defensive leverage of the opposition. Anything that brings more of your resources to bear at the crucial point is good; anything that brings more of your opponent's resources into the fray is bad. That is why the Dardanelles campaign during the First World War, when British and Empire forces assaulted the Turkish controlled access to the Black Sea is considered such a strategic blunder – not because the campaign was ultimately unsuccessful and costly, but because Turkish units that would not otherwise have been involved in the war ended up tying down lots of allied forces that could otherwise have been used elsewhere.

Strategic thinking can also drive actions of the defensive player. Ideally you want to persuade an aggressor that it is not worth their while attacking by effecting their cost-benefit analysis. This can be achieved in three ways: (1) Through increasing the costs of their attack; (2) Through threatening massive retaliation; (3) Through making the potential fruits of victory less appealing. The first of these strategic acts involves defensive measures, such as building fortifications, mustering forces that look forbiddingly strong, or in terms of the marketplace, making sure that you are well financed, and so likely to be able to survive a price war.

The second is called deterrence. In contrast to dissuasion by defense, dissuasion by deterrence operates by frightening an opponent out of attacking, not because of the difficulty of launching an attack and carrying it home, but because the expected reaction of the attacked will result in one's own severe punishment. Defense and deterrence are often confused. Nuclear deterrence is the most obvious international form, but it can also be found in legal battles with every threatened suit matched with a threatened counter-suit, and in the marketplace where corporations and countries routinely threaten dire recriminations for acts seen as hostile.

The third is called a 'scorched earth' policy, whereby the retreating defender destroys everything of value to the aggressor. This could involve burning your fields in the face of an advancing army, or burdening your company with debt, pension schemes or union agreements in order to make it less appealing for a hostile takeover. The dangers of such a policy are that whatever happens, your own utility will be harmed – either you do enough damage to your own resources for them to no longer attract the interest of hostiles, or worse, you do a great deal of damage to your resources, but nevertheless it is not sufficient to put off hostile interest and you are taken over anyway.

### *2.4.2 Look before You Leap*

Strategic thinking requires that you look beyond the immediate costs and benefits of your actions towards the longer term implications. Failure to do so can not only result in a future where you are actually worse off (thereby rendering your initial action irrational), but can also result in you not being able to extricate yourself from the disadvantageous position. The causes of this situation are 'sunk costs' and 'entrapment.'

Sunk costs are very familiar to gamblers. After losing a

substantial amount of money, an individual may feel that the situation can only be rectified by a larger wager at the next betting opportunity. Many have found themselves destitute as a result of such a policy of throwing good money after bad. The same sort of reasoning can be found in international financial and investment markets and international business. Nick Leeson, the infamous 'Rogue Trader' who caused the collapse of Barings Bank followed such reasoning in trying to recover his position from disastrous early trades. Likewise, multinational corporations can waste millions pouring money into underperforming subsidiaries or trying to promote unpopular 'turkeys,' as can governments subsidizing failing national industries.

If the sunk costs are sufficiently large, it can become literally impossible to withdraw from the disastrous position. The sunk costs will have been sufficient to 'entrap' you by changing your rational payoffs. United States involvement in the Vietnam War is a prime example of this. It became quickly apparent that the conflict in Southeast Asia was not going to produce a good outcome for the US in cost-benefit terms, but at every turn, because of the amount already invested in terms of money, material, prestige, and human lives, the choice was made by successive Presidents and military commanders to actually pump more resources in and escalate the conflict rather than to cut their losses and pull out. It could be argued that a similar problem now faces the United States with regard to Iraq.

In all these cases, if decision-makers had looked before they leapt, had considered the long term strategic implications of their actions, they might have decided on a different course of action. At the very least they might have considered a different allocation of resources at the onset of the crisis rather than a gradual escalation, with each increment proving insufficient to deal with the escalating costs. The

Iraq quagmire may have been avoidable had sufficient forces been committed at the onset of the campaign. Likewise independent reports into the Rwandan genocide have confirmed what was initially claimed by the United Nations commander on the ground, that a relatively small UN force, with an increased mandate to take decisive action could have averted one of the greatest humanitarian catastrophes of the twentieth century.

Unfortunately, often the true costs of our actions only become known with hindsight, and it takes a bold decision-maker to commit more of his or her resources to an operation than at first sight seems necessary for success. Usually there is a great deal of pressure upon decision-makers to generate the maximum possible returns for the minimum investment of scarce resources. Democracies are in fact particularly susceptible to these problems, partly because of public pressure on decision-makers to minimize costs and/or body bags; and in part because democracies are led by officials elected for short and often finite terms whose strategic vision is naturally truncated to that of the next election, or the end of their term in office.

### *2.4.3 Nash Equilibria*

In game theory, a Nash equilibrium (named after John Nash) is a situation which emerges in any game involving two or more players, where no player has anything to gain by changing his or her own strategy assuming that the strategies of other players remain constant. Equilibria stay stable under successive rounds of 'I think that he thinks…etc.' Each has correctly predicted the other's action and has chosen his own best response. This is not necessarily the best position for all, but the one that under rational conditions remains stable. If nothing you do will result in a better payoff, then you have no incentive to change your course of action. If this is true for all actors, then nobody will change their courses of action, hence an equilibrium ensues.

It is important to note that there may be more than one such equilibrium for any game. Alternatively there may be no equilibria at all, just a constant series of strategic interactions. An example of the former may be industry standardization of format for a new technology (the emerging struggle between Blue-ray and HD-DVD for the next generation of video storage and reproduction is in fact a struggle over the establishment of the new industry standard, as was that between Betamax and the ultimately victorious VHS). It is in the interests of all the producers of the new technology to agree to a standardized format (as this will maximize the market and lead to economies of scale), but it does not really matter which format is adopted as even the worst off producer is better off with the standardized format that gives them the lowest yield returns than they would be with no standardization. In this game there will be as many Nash equilibria as there are potential standardized formats.

Likewise, we may all have slight preferences for driving on one side of the road or the other, but these preferences pale into insignificance compared to the massive disincentives (head-on crashes) that exist if we do not reach agreement on which side of the road upon which to drive. Thus all parties driving on the left, or all parties driving on the right both form a Nash equilibrium, as no party has sufficient incentive to change and drive on the other side of the road once the equilibrium has been put into place. Figure 2.1 is a payoff matrix demonstrating graphically this simple game. The payoffs for each driver are abstracts of utility or symbolic representation of the amount of 'good' each receives under given conditions.

**<Figure 2.1> Payoff Marix for the Driving Game and Nash Equilibria**

| | | **Driver A** | |
|---|---|---|---|
| **Driver B** | | Drive on the Left | Drive on the Right |
| | Drive on the Left | 100, 100 | 0, 0 |
| | Drive on the Right | 0, 0 | 100, 100 |

If we all drive on the left, *or* we all drive on the right, we all gain the utility of avoiding head-on crashes, rightly given the very large figure of +100 to each party in the matrix above. If however we choose unilaterally to change the side upon which we drive then everybody ends up with zero utility – nobody gains anything because we all end up dying from head-on collisions.

In all of these examples, the dominant strategies for all players (those that provide better payoffs in all circumstances) are those that should lead to cooperation (albeit after an initial struggle over which side of the road on which to drive, or which format to accept as the industry standard) whereas the dominated strategies of all players (those that are worse under all conditions) are those that relate to conflictual behavior. However, some strategic conditions result in games where the dominant strategy for all players leads to conflict rather than cooperation. The most famous of these is termed the prisoner's dilemma.

### *2.4.4 The Prisoner's Dilemma*

In the prisoner's dilemma, two accomplices caught committing a minor crime are suspected of a more serious offence. They are therefore separated and each offered the incentive of amnesty for the crime they are undoubtedly guilty of in return for a confession implicating the other in the larger offence. If neither confesses, both go to prison for a short period of time (say two years). If one confesses and the other does not, then one walks free, and the other endures a much longer stint behind bars (say ten years). If both confess implicating each other, then both go to prison for the bigger job, although they will get some time off for cooperating with the police (say eight years). Maximum utility for the prisoners (together) would be achieved if they both remained silent (two years each). This would be considered the Pareto-optimal solution. Figure 2.2 is a payoff matrix for the prisoner's dilemma, where scores represent years in prison rather than utility and therefore larger scores represent lower utility.

**<Figure 2.2> The Prisoner's Dilemma**

| | Prisoner A | | |
|---|---|---|---|
| **Prisoner B** | | Stay Silent | Defect/Betray |
| | Stay Silent | 2, 2 | 10, 0 |
| | Defect/Betray | 0, 10 | 8, 8 |

However, there are rational incentives for them to defect. In fact, no matter what the other does, it is best for each prisoner to betray the other or to 'defect.' If 'A' defects and 'B' stays silent then 'A' is free. If 'A' defects and so does 'B', then they both go down for eight years, but had 'A' not defected, then she would have gone down for ten years. Unfortunately, with both of them following this logic, both will end up serving eight years instead of the two each that they could gain from cooperating.

Figure 2.3 (below) represents the payoff matrix for each of the prisoners in order to identify their dominant strategy. As we can see, if a prisoner stays silent their payoff will be either 2 or 10 years, whereas if they defect the payoff will be either 0 or 8 years. Hence, in a single playing of this game where the prisoners are not allowed to communicate with each other during the game, defection is the optimum or dominant strategy for both players and the equilibrium is actually mutual betrayal rather than the Pareto-optimal mutual silence.

**<Figure 2.3> Prisoner Payoff Matrix**

| | Payoff | | |
|---|---|---|---|
| | | Rival Stays Silent | Rival Defects |
| **Prisoner A or B** | Stay Silent | -2 | -10 |
| | Defect/Betray | 0 | -8 |

The initial circumstances that prevent a Pareto-optimal solution are that the two prisoners have been separated from each other and are unable to communicate to discus what their best cooperative strategy might be. However, even if they were able to communicate, this would still not guarantee cooperation, as how can each prisoner be sure that the other will keep his word once given? Is there really honor among thieves? A lack of trust is what ultimately guarantees the mutual defection and a worse outcome for both than might otherwise be achieved.

In international politics, political realists identify the international arena as being akin to a prisoner's dilemma. The reasoning goes that if states are sovereign that means they answer to no higher authority. This in turn means that even if interests are shared, cooperation is unlikely and should not be relied upon for the provision of national security and defense. Rather, each state must rely on self-help, with the strong doing what they want and the weak suffering what they must. Consequently each state will seek to maximize its military capabilities, even if the money so used would be better spent on welfare, infrastructure, or development. Thus all states end up worse off by being forced to maximize their spending on weapons even though all states would be better off if none were possessed. This is particularly true when all military spending by one state, even if defensive in nature, is seen as a threat by its neighbors and rivals, and thus tends to be countered through a process of arms racing.

Yet the shortcoming of the prisoner's dilemma can be overcome. One solution is that those who play such games may ultimately become 'super-rational' by which is meant that even if the 'rational' policy leads to mutual defection, both sides will realize this, and will realize (and expect) that the other side will realize this making it a self-denying prophecy. They may also know that in a symmetrical game there exists a Pareto-optimal solution as well as the disastrous mutual defection scenario, and will therefore chose to cooperate while expecting the other to do likewise. This double or even triple thinking is similar to what Nigel Howard has termed 'meta-games' wherein the decision is not made as a case analysis of what the opponent does, but dependent on the strategy the opponent follows (1971). However, here we may be overemphasizing the 'theoretical' part of international negotiation theory, and there are a number of more pragmatic ways to overcome the dilemma.

Liberal and neoliberal approaches to international studies emphasize that real world international negotiations do not take place under conditions that are likely to generate a prisoner's dilemma. First of all, rather than each side being unable to communicate with the others, international actors in fact engage in a continuous dialogue with each other through multiple channels of communication. Secondly, rather than the one shot strategic interaction characterized by the classic prisoner's dilemma, international negotiations are in fact a series of strategic interactions over time conducted between the same players – sometimes called an 'iterated' game.

The incentives are considerably changed if the game is played repeatedly over time. Through communication and repeated interaction the parties may establish a cooperative culture. Even if this is not the case, all parties have opportunities to punish defectors in future interactions in a 'tit-for-tat' manner, or to reward cooperative behavior. This is sometimes referred to as 'enlarging the shadow of the future,' and may lead to cooperative behavior through making interactions more durable, more frequent, or both (Axelrod 1984, 129).

Thus while one might gain by abusing the other's trust in the single-shot version, on a repeated playing, the other would not trust them and so would also defect in the second round. As both parties know this, there is an incentive not to defect. One party to a treaty, trade agreement, business transaction, etc, might break it, but would undoubtedly find it harder to negotiate with other actors in the future as their reputation would suffer and this would leave them in a situation both absolutely worse off with regard to their optimal outcome, and relatively worse of with regard to other players in the competitive game who chose to cooperate.

Other solutions to the prisoner's dilemma include external punishment for defection from outside the parameters of the game. Rather than the tit-for-tat disincentives to defection meted out by other payers, an external body (a leviathan, a court, an international organization, international law, etc) could be entitled and/or enabled to enforce cooperation and punish defection. The operations of external agencies can also, therefore, effectively change the payoffs. In fact, according to Axelrod, 'getting out of Prisoner's Dilemmas is one the primary functions of government' (1984, 133). Even in our classic example above, if our two prisoners both belonged to the Mafia, the code of *omerta* (silence) may well be enough to prevent defection, either because each prisoner is aware they would probably not live to enjoy the freedom won at the expense of their accomplice, or because they place great store upon the normative value of the code itself and what it represents.

### *2.4.5 The Stag Hunt or Trust Dilemma Game*

The Genevan-French philosopher, Jean Jacques Rousseau, first introduced us to another set of strategic considerations under which an individual may have a rational imperative to pursue his own interests rather than cooperate with one or more others, even if his selfishness will ultimately result in a lower individual payoff. Many of the logical conditions that apply to the prisoner's dilemma also apply to the Stag Hunt or Trust Dilemma game.

Consider a situation where two (or more) hunters are required jointly to hunt a stag (a large adult male deer), but where each can easily hunt a hare (sometimes depicted as a rabbit). Even a shared portion of venison (deer meat) is superior in both quantity and quality to what is to be found on a hare, but the stag can only be brought down through cooperation between all the hunters. Thus hunting stags is most beneficial collectively but requires a lot of trust among the hunters that each will not be distracted by any tasty and easy meal that crosses his path (hares) thereby letting the stag escape through a hole in the line.

In particular, there is a danger that if one hunter decides to go for the greater good (cooperates) while the other goes for the hare (defects), then the first hunter will get nothing, whereas the second will at least get something in his belly. In this game mutual cooperation is a Pareto-optimal Nash equilibrium. Under all conditions, stag is better than hare, so your dominant strategy should be to go for stag. However, temptation to defect arises when you believe that others will defect because you have reason to doubt the rationality or integrity of others, or in groups large enough that, given the vagaries of human nature, some defections are likely. Where there is doubt or distrust, it is likely that each hunter will go after the sure thing rather than go hungry. Figure 2.4 is a sample payoff matrix for the Stag Hunt.

**<Figure 2.4> The Stag Hunt**

| | **Hunter A** | | |
|---|---|---|---|
| **Hunter B** | | Stag | Hare |
| | Stag | 10, 10 | 0, 7 |
| | Hare | 7, 0 | 7, 7 |

In fact there are two pure Nash equilibria in this game – either both hunters will go for the Pareto-optimal solution of Stag, or if they cannot trust the other sufficiently, or are unsure about their rationality, they will both go for hare. The first equilibrium is payoff dominant (Pareto-optimal), whereas the second is risk dominant (known as Hicks-optimal). Whether in any given strategic situation the hunters go for maximizing payoffs or minimizing risks depends on the operating conditions (degree of trust, enforcement, relationship, repeated interactions between the players etc) and also upon the personalities of the hunters themselves – are they risk averse or risk takers? Pessimists or those with a cynical view of human nature will always hunt hare, whereas optimists will hunt stag.

Solutions to the stag hunt or trust dilemma game are similar to those of the prisoner's dilemma – meta-games, iterated games, tit-for-tat internal enforcement, or leviathan or judicial external enforcement. However, as already mentioned, not all simultaneous move games have equilibria of the type encountered in the prisoner's dilemma and the stag hunt. In the next model we explore some of the rational implications of having each individual's dominant strategy being determined by the likely actions of the other player.

### *2.4.6 Chicken*

We are probably all familiar with the game of chicken from Hollywood movies, or even (one would hope in a far less dangerous form) from our own experience. In the movie version, two rebellious teenagers drive cars directly towards each other at breakneck speed. Whoever swerves first is the chicken; whoever stays the course is the hero. If both stay the course, we are left with two dead heroes – by most measures of utility a particularly bad situation. Maximum utility is achieved for any one player when he sticks the course but the other chickens out. In between these two situations, in decreasing order of utility there are the scenarios of both chickening out, and chickening out when the other stays the course. Chicken payoffs are modeled in figure 2.5.

**<Figure 2.5> Chicken**

| | | **Rebel A** | |
|---|---|---|---|
| **Rebel B** | | Swerve | Straight |
| | Swerve | -5, -5 | -10, 10 |
| | Straight | 10, -10 | -100, -100 |

If Rebel A and Rebel B both swerve, they both lose face (and probably damage their cars driving into a ditch). Yet this is nothing compared to the loss of utility (and probably life) if neither of the drivers swerve, and they drive straight into each other. If Rebel A drives straight and Rebel B swerves, the former is a hero (at least for a day) and gains considerable utility, whereas the latter not only loses face and ends up in a ditch, but also suffers by comparison (and therefore in relative utility terms) with Rebel A. Obviously, if the positions are reversed, so are the payoffs.

The game of chicken is similar in many ways to that of the

prisoner's dilemma and the stag hunt. However, unlike the prisoner's dilemma at all times, and the stag hunt under conditions of low trust, the players do not have a dominant strategy of defection. Yet neither do they have a dominant strategy of cooperation, unlike the iterated prisoner's dilemma or a stag hunt under conditions of high trust. Rather, each player's strategy is dependent upon that of his rival – each must try to calculate the other's degree of resolve and push the game one step further than can be endured by their opponent in order to maximize utility.

There are no obvious solutions to this game other than perhaps not to play it! However, any player who even suggests that it may be best not to engage upon such a foolhardy course of action becomes an instant loser in terms of utility, as it looks as if he is chickening out before the game has even started. Only the actions of an external agent, such as a law enforcement officer can adequately defend the players from the consequences of their own actions.

In terms of increasing the likelihood of 'winning' a game of chicken, the key is to convince the other party that you are truly irrational enough to risk absolute disaster. Perhaps this could be made more believable by demonstrating to the other party that you are completely crazy. It could be argued, for instance, that weapons of mass destruction only work to coerce others if you can convince them that you are mad enough to use them. Thus generating a reputation for total irrationality can also be seen as on occasion being very rational. This is probably the reasoning behind the reputation of President Kim Jong-Il of North Korea for wily negotiation (Howe 2003).

Alternatively, it may be possible to convince the other party of your irrevocable commitment to a certain course of action. In our driving analogy this could be achieved by throwing your steering wheel out of the car, thereby making it impossible for you to swerve, and effectively turning a simultaneous game into a sequential game. In international negotiations, this is often attempted through demonstrating how little freedom of movement you have to negotiate due to difficulties in selling any agreement to internal constituencies back home, thereby turning a potential weakness into a position of strength.

All the games we have so far considered are essentially 'simultaneous' games wherein each player must make his move at the same time, or without explicit knowledge or the moves of others. Rational considerations change considerably when explored under conditions of sequential decision-making, whereby each decision-maker has a chance to respond strategically to the prior moves of his opponent. The next section considers decision-making during sequential move games.

## 2.5 Sequential Games

In a sequential game, a single actor (Actor 1) must choose between 'A' and 'B' (or sometimes many other options). His future actions are then dependent on his initial choice. Thus if he chose 'A' he is then only free to chose 'C' or 'D,' whereas if he chose 'B' he is then only free to chose 'E' or 'F.' For instance, certain postgraduate courses may only be open to those with a fairly limited number of undergraduate majors. If you have taken an undergraduate degree with a different major, then these courses will not be available to you to choose upon graduation. Likewise, many jobs require particular graduate qualifications.

If you do not or cannot take specific graduate qualifications, certain career choices may not be available to you once you finish your studies. It therefore makes sense to look forward to your ultimate goal and then reason backwards to the decisions you must make to put you on the correct path. Figure 2.6 is a graphical representation of such a thought process. Note that only two possible majors and subsequent career paths are shown. In reality, or course, many more majors can be chosen, and thus your decision-tree is likely to be far more complex than this simple model.

**<Figure 2.6> Decision-Making Tree: The Impact of High School Choices**

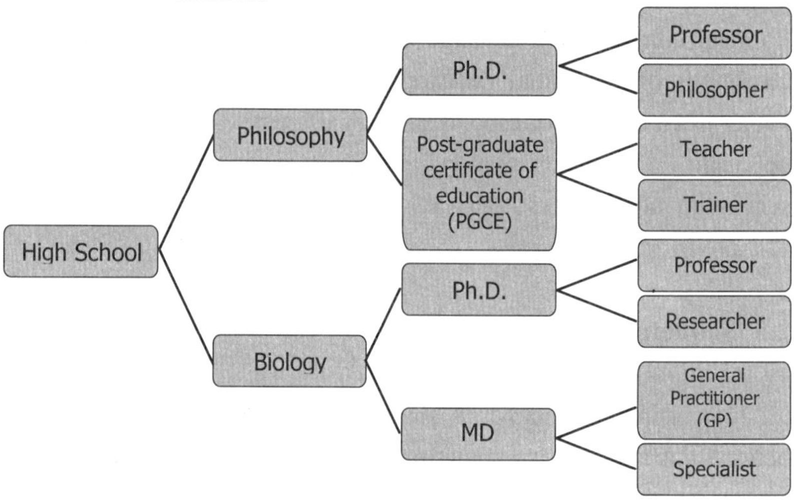


Again, things get a little more complicated when the decision-making processes of more than one individual are considered. In multi-actor sequential decision-making, based upon the impact of Actor 1's decision, Actor two must then make his own rational decision between a number of options. If Actor 1 chose 'A' then Actor 2 may chose 'C' or 'D.' If Actor 1 chose 'B' then Actor 2 may chose 'E' or 'F,' and so on. For Dixit and Nalebuf, 'the general principle for sequential-move games is that each player should figure out the other player's future responses, and use them in calculating his own best current move' and that this idea is so important that it is worth codifying into a basic rule of strategic behavior: 'Look ahead and reason back' (1991). Figure 2.7 is a decision-tree for a two actor sequential decision-making game involving a bully and his victim.

**<Figure 2.7> Decision-Making Tree: The Bullying Game**

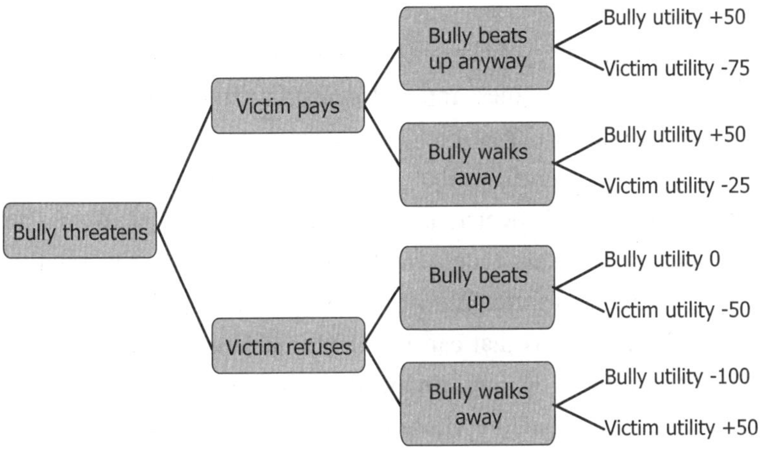


It will be noted that in the bullying game (above) there are actually only two possible outcomes – either the bully caries out his threat or he walks away. However, depending on the sequential decision-making of the victim, payoffs and their probability of occurring could nevertheless be radically different. The beating administered if the victim does pay could be much less severe than if he doesn't pay. There could also be less likelihood of the bully making the decision to beat the victim up if the victim pays. On the other hand, standing up to a bully and making the bully back down is the best possible outcome for the victim, resulting in a much higher utility than any of the other outcomes, and even standing up to a bully but getting beaten up may be preferable to the outcomes listed should the victim decide to pay.

The payoffs could also alter for the bully. His best outcome is to get the money (whether this includes a post-extortion beating depends on his level of sadism, boredom, energy, chance of being caught, etc). However, if the victim refuses to pay, it is not so clear whether the bully should carry out his threat. If he does, then he could actually lose the fight, he could get into trouble with the authorities, and at the very least, he will have to exert himself. If however he walks away, his reputation will be severely damaged.

In all sequential games, rational decision-making depends upon the impact of two variables: First, the difference in expected payoffs; and second; the probability that a particular result will occur as a result of the initial decision. For example, when applying to universities, a rational student will consider not only the relative merits of studying at different institutions, but also, given the limited number of applications that can be submitted (due to administrative constraints in the UK and financial constraints in the US), the relative likelihood that the chosen institutions will indeed give an offer of a place to the applicant. If we insert probabilities based on payoffs into the bullying decision-tree, we get a clearer picture of what the victim should do. (See Figure 2.8).

For the victim, if he pays he will have a 25% chance of being beaten up and thus receiving a utility of -75 and a 75% chance of being let go and receiving a utility of 'only' -25. This will give an average utility of -75(.25) + -25(.75) = -18.75 + -18.75 = -37.5. If, however, he does not pay, because the expected utility for the bully is so much worse if he does not carry out his threat, he should expect a beating. Therefore his average utility will be -50(.90) + 50(.10) = -45 + 5 = -40. Thus under these conditions, unless the prospective victim is particularly heroic, principled, or foolhardy, it probably makes sense for him to pay up. If the bully is able to calculate this, it will give him an added incentive to extort money, because he will know that in most cases the prospective victim will pay up if the victim is likely to make the same cost-benefits calculus.

**<Figure 2.8> The Bullying Game with Known Probabilities**

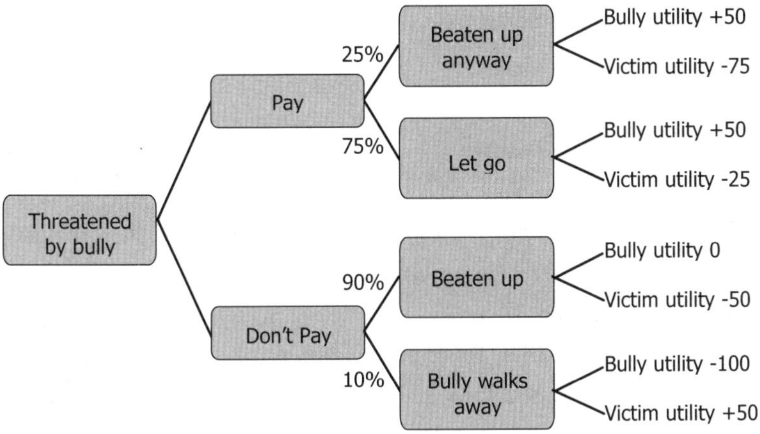


Incentives to reach agreement in sequential games can include increasing costs or decreasing returns over time. For example, two parties locked in a dispute will often have to pay lawyers. The longer the dispute continues, the more each party has to pay their lawyers, thus there will come a time that the additional benefit you will be able to hustle out of the other side through a protracted negotiation may well get more than eaten up by your extra costs. Alternatively, the value of the disputed item may decline over time – an argument over distribution of profits regarding a perishable commodity runs the risk of even the winning side getting less than had a settlement been reached earlier. Getting all of nothing is winning the battle but losing the war, or cutting your nose to spite your face.

For the principle of looking ahead and reasoning back to apply, it is essential that earlier moves be observable to those who choose later, otherwise all parties run the risk of becoming caught up in an inescapable net of second guessing. Indeed, when earlier moves are not observable to those who chose later, even if chronologically the moves take place sequentially, in rational terms we have reverted to what is essentially a simultaneous-move game. The observability of the moves of other actors is one of the important real world constraints on international negotiations dealt with in the next section.

## 2.6 Real World Limitations

This chapter has dealt with the theoretical underpinnings that are applied in international negotiations with regard to the bases of rationality and game theory. Unfortunately, as we have already alluded to in this chapter, there are a number of shortcomings when such models are applied to real world analysis of international negotiations. The fundamental problem is that while these models work well when applied to unitary rational actors (similar to individual human beings), the complexity of the entities which engage in international negotiations means that they often appear neither rational nor unitary.

On the question of rationality, sometimes it is just not worth the effort to engage in the sort of mental gymnastics mentioned above. In other words, it may not be rational to think rationally as the costs involved in gaining the information necessary for a rational decision outweigh any potential benefits. There may be a slight advantage in getting out of one side of bed rather than the other, but we are unlikely to make such calculations before putting our feet on the floor. Alternatively, it may not be 'strategic' to engage in rational actions. Rationality breeds predictability, and on occasion it may be rational to engage in an irrational course of action precisely because this is unexpected.

Larger problems related to rationality concern inherent assumptions such as: perfect information about the payoffs to other players (we may not know what constitutes their hierarchy of preferences); not discounting future utility too heavily (we have already noted how politicians tend to look at short term rather than long term gains); knowledge of all the other player's moves at all times (again, as mentioned above, we may not be able to observe all or any of their actions); interpersonal utility (individuals and groups may vary on the amount of utility they place upon different outcomes – personality and culture can often play a role); and the ability to play without making any mistakes. These are all problematic in the international environment. Indeed, the theory of 'hyper-games' explores scenarios in which the adversaries have different conceptions of what 'the game' is, and thus the standard rational and mathematical modeling of game theory does not apply, and the sides may take apparently paradoxical actions.

On the question of unitary decision-making, many of the entities we deal with in international negotiations (such as states, multinational corporations, and international organizations) are exceedingly complex entities with numerous sources of input for policy formulation. Each part of the complex whole may have a different set of preferences and payoffs, and the eventual policy that is produced may be the result of a compromise or aggregation of these individual inputs that does not conform to our simple concept of hierarchies of preferences and cost-benefit analyses. Perhaps most importantly, much of the simple modeling presented above is only really suitable for analyzing two-party cooperation. In a multi-party environment such as the international community, we need to look at a more complex model.

Thus in the next chapter we shall turn to considerations of the impact of perceptions on international negotiations, the problem of communication, the impact of decision-making structure and operating environment (two-level games, feedback, etc), and n-person analysis (or multi-player games).

## References

Axelrod, Robert. 1984. *The Evolution of Cooperation*. New York: Basic Books.

Bates, Robert, Avner Greif, Margaret Levi, Jean-Laurent Rosenthal, Barry R Weingast. 1998. *Analytic Narratives*. Princeton: Princeton University Press.

Dixit, Avinash K. and Barry J. Nalebuff. 1991. *Thinking Strategically*. New York: Norton & Company.

Howard, Nigel. 1971. *Paradoxes of Rationality: theory of metagames and irrational behavior*. Cambridge: MIT Press.

Howe, Brendan. 2003. 'Reengaging the North: War or Peace in Northeast Asia?' *Korean Journal of Defense Analysis* Vol. XV, No. 2. Seoul: Korea Institute of Defense Analysis, Fall 2003 pp 199-221.

Verba, S. 1969. 'Assumptions of Rationality and Non-Rationality in Models of the International System' in J.N. Rosenau (ed.), *International Politics and Foreign Policy*. New York: Free Press.

# Chapter 3 International Negotiations Practical Dilemmas

## 3.1 Introduction

In the previous chapter we examined some of the theoretical principles underlying the analysis of decision-making in international negotiations. These include the concepts of rationality, unitary decision-making, utility maximization, dominant strategies, strategic decision-making, payoffs and equilibria. Such assumptions and the game theoretical models based upon them have helped shape 'real world' international negotiation policy formulation.

In the first part of this chapter we will examine the Rational Actor Model (RAM) of foreign policy decision-making which heavily influenced practitioners during the Cold War. However, as mentioned in the previous chapter, this model (including its underlying assumptions) falls short of incorporating all the complexities of contemporary world international negotiations. Thus later in this chapter we will examine the shortcomings of RAM, and also some of the more complex models that have been introduced to overcome those shortcomings.

## 3.2 The Rational Actor Model

Traditionally, in studying foreign policy decision-making, analysts have tended to focus on the role of the state, and upon the governing elite of statesmen at the helm of each of these geographically bounded political entities. Much theoretical modelling in the fields of international business and international trade has also tended to take a similar unitary view of decision-making, focusing on distinct corporate entities or their chief executive officers (CEOs). It is from this starting point that Graham Allison began his classic work *Essence of Decision* (1971).

The first model of decision-making that Allison addresses is the rational actor model (RAM), which adopts the view of the state as unitary rational actor - i.e. a single indivisible entity (similar to an individual human being) that makes choices on the basis of rational application of cost/benefit analysis with regard to a hierarchy of values and preferred outcomes. These choices are used in order to promote solutions to strategic problems with regard to maximizing utility, minimizing cost and achieving strategic goals. This leads to a 'conception of international politics as essentially bargaining situations' in which alert, intelligent, coordinated nations speak and move in order to influence other nations by changing their expected payoffs (Allison 1971, 22).

The influence of individual preferences, perceptions, and morality is minimized by emphasizing the importance of the *state as actor* within this concept. If statesmen are rational and act in accordance with the needs of the society and national interest, then no matter who is at the helm, the ship will be steered in the same direction. Rational decision-makers are expected to construct a hierarchy of preferred outcomes and then conduct a simple cost-benefit analysis (in terms of national interest and resources) in order to determine which course of action to take. Hence the complexities of the decision-making process are simplified through the concept of a 'black box of decision' as represented in figure 3.1.

**<Figure 3.1> Rational Actor Model**

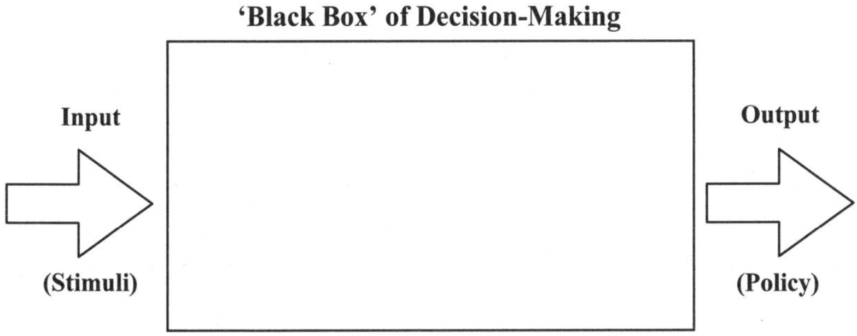


The game theoretical models examined in the previous chapter, such as prisoner's dilemma, stag hunt, or chicken are directly applicable under such conditions. However, the limitations of both the rational actor model and the associated game theoretical models have also been extensively documented. In the following sections we will examine such shortcomings and alternative models that have been proposed by theorists in order to address them.

## 3.3 The Tragedy of the Commons and Collective Action Problems

Some of the models examined above are mostly suitable for two-party or very limited multi-party negotiations. Yet in the modern international arena negotiations often involve large numbers of participants. Indeed, multilateral international negotiations have become the norm. Thus a more complex model is required. In an article for *Science* in 1968 Garrett Hardin developed and popularized another more sophisticated rational model for use in explaining collective action problems (Hardin 1968). The tragedy of the commons may be seen as something of a multi-lateral or n-person prisoner's dilemma.

In this model, a number of owners of livestock graze their animals on common (public) land. As the grazing is essentially free, and the benefits of raising livestock considerable, the incentive for all is to raise as many animals on the common land as possible. Unfortunately the common land can only support a finite number of animals. Hence, if there are too many animals on the common land there will not be enough grass to support them and some or all of the animals will die. Thus all of the owners might agree voluntarily to restrict the numbers they put on the land (albeit after a famine or two).

This scenario introduces new elements to the problems of cooperation in an anarchic society (that is to say, a community where rules are only enforced through consent) such as the international community. It is rational here for the group as a whole to agree to limit their flocks or herds for the collective good. If all overgraze then the land is ruined. But if the group is sufficiently large, it might be difficult 1) to identify if a single individual has chosen not to follow the rules and defect (assuming that one extra animal will not make a significant difference), and 2) to determine who is guilty of defection.

Furthermore, if one defects, it might still be rational for others to continue to cooperate and allow individuals to defect up to the point that one more free-rider would cause the collapse of the collective action (this individual would be the pivotal member of the group) given that whole-scale defection would lead to ruin for all. Michael Laver points out that, knowing this, defection (betrayal) and free-riding (attempting to gain all the benefits of cooperation without bearing the costs) become attractive once more, even in repeat-play or iterated games (1997, 61). Every rational member of the group will attempt to become a tolerated free-rider (a free-rider whose defection is not pivotal to the breakdown of cooperation). Indeed it is likely that there will be a stampede to defect, and collective action will collapse.

It is hard for the group as a whole convincingly to threaten to punish defectors and thereby coerce free-riders to follow the rules. A credible threat must involve more than merely implementing the rules of the game in a tit-for-tat manner if it is to change game play. The problem is that imposing severe sanctions on those who break the rules also imposes further costs on the law abiders who must pay the cost of detecting and punishing the violators. Thus, threats to punish violators are often likely to be seen as unbelievable because potential violators are aware that the law-abiders do not want to pay the often high costs of implementing a regime of detection and punishment.

In particular, this scenario endangers cooperation in the international community where the costs of coercion are very high and the number of actors fairly large. However, that there has been a degree of cooperation and collective action in the international community suggests that there are ways in which the collective action problem may be surmounted. The following section considers solutions to the collective action problem.

## 3.4 Potential Solutions to the Problems of Collective Action[1]

### *3.4.1 Exclusion*

The first solution would be to throw free riders out of the

[1] Much of section 3.4 and its subsections is taken from and explored in more detail by: Brendan Howe, 'Rationality and Intervention in an Anarchic Society' *Korean Journal of Defense Analysis* Vol. 18, No. 1 (Korea Institute of Defense Analysis, Spring 2006) pp 161-185.

community, excluding them from collective benefits as they refuse to pay any of the costs. However, it is impossible or at least not cost effective, to exclude from some collective benefits those who do not contribute to their production. For example, it is not possible to prevent free-riders who continue to produce CFCs from enjoying an improved layer of ozone protection. Likewise, it might not be cost effective to keep trade restricting practices in place purely for those who defect from the terms of a free trade pact. Thus, as pointed out by Laver, 'in short, for technical and/or economic reasons, many collective consumption goods cannot feasibly be "privatized"'(1997, 40).

### *3.4.2 Enforcement*

A further potential solution is that of enforcement. In domestic negotiations, the problem of free-riders can, to a great extent, be mitigated by recourse to the courts. The problem in international negotiations is that, while there are international courts of adjudication and arbitration, international law is essentially consensual – states must agree to submit disputes to the courts, and also agree to be bound by their decision. Unlike domestic courts, international courts do not have compulsory jurisdiction. In addition, while domestically we might appeal to the police to protect our interests against unscrupulous neighbors, that option is not available in the international environment where there is no global police force.

### *3.4.3 Leviathan*

Thomas Hobbes, the English philosopher proposed another, related solution to the problem of collective action in his concept of a 'Leviathan,' an entity with overwhelming power that compels individuals to play fair. With the end of the Cold War, the single remaining super-power, America, could be viewed as holding such a position in international politics, and that American hegemony has created an environment conducive to international cooperation. The US, so it could be argued, has the power to enforce agreements and compliance with international law. Thus participating in collective action has become rational as it costs more to back out than to comply, resulting in the elimination of free-riders.

However, there are a number of problems with this approach. First, the US does not hold anywhere near enough power to be considered an international leviathan - the leviathan must be a virtual dictator acting beyond the law and not subject to it. Again, as pointed out by Laver:

> Since the power to enforce agreements is unqualified by any countervailing obligation, and since the monarch is not a party to the agreement that grants this power, the monarch is in effect a dictator. This is logically necessary for Hobbes's solution since, if there is a power to enforce some obligation on the monarch, *then the monarch is not a monarch*' (1997, 43).

Second, and perhaps most importantly, it would not be rational for other states to cooperate in being bound by one of their number. Why would rational actors, in Locke's terminology, agree to be devoured by the Lion in order that they may be safeguarded from the Pole-Cats and Foxes? Finally, if it were rational to opt out of the costs of rule-enforcement and punishment of free riders, why would the United States agree to take on such a burden?

### *3.4.4 Political Entrepreneurship*

There are two possible rational actor models that can be used to explain this conundrum. First, we can view organizations that provide leadership as political entrepreneurs. A political entrepreneur holds insufficient coercive resources to subjugate the group as a whole, but enough to deal with small rogue groups or free-riders. They provide, for reward, '"political services" that help the group resolve their collective action problems' (Laver 1997, 86-71). The portfolio of political services provided is termed the regime. The regime either produces public goods directly or facilitates their production by private individuals or groups through the resolution of certain collective action problems.

Under such conditions, it may well be rational for states to agree to be bound by the hegemon in order to resolve some of their collective action problems, and indeed it is on this sort of reasoning that regime theory rests. What we have yet to explain is that, given all these restraints, and the massive costs involved, why would any hegemon agree to take on the role of a political entrepreneur? Why not just continue to play the role of the strongest player in an anarchic society based on self-help? The basic answer to this question is that by acting in such a way the hegemon is able to ensure the production of a package of political services and collective goods that they privately prefer to what would emerge if they didn't get involved.

However, this being the case, it would also make sense to bind together with other entrepreneurs in order to spread costs, and maybe allow tendering for a far larger package of political services and collective good production. This leads on to the second new rational model, that of hegemonic coalitions.

### *3.4.5 Hegemonic Coalitions*

A number of scenarios could lead to this model of behavior in international society. An ambitious entrepreneur could look to achieve results beyond the scope of its individual powers. A declining hegemon could look to spread the costs of maintaining the regime, or silence troublesome critics by giving them a slice of the action and a share of the responsibility. Or we could perceive other states as junior entrepreneurial partners in the regime rather than merely the public for whom the political services are provided.

For all members of the coalition there is the potential of a gain in aggregate bargaining power, influence and collective good production. For the senior partner there is a reduction of costs of the sort mentioned above. Although a share of the profits of incumbency must be given up, this is made up for by the expected higher probability of winning future contracts and the chance of silencing critics. For the junior partners the prospects of future exclusive incumbency is ceded in exchange for a more certain but less valuable part of the benefits of the current incumbent's office.

The likelihood of such an alliance is greatly increased if the interests and policies of the various partners are closely aligned. In order to promote a stable coalition for maintaining the status quo, it is important that all parties are clear about the policies that are to be followed by the incumbency. It only makes sense for a junior partner to support the leader if it is likely to promote interests common to both. The leader may feel inclined to defect from the promises made to gain the support of junior partners, but then the regime would soon disintegrate.

### *3.4.6 Reputation*

Here we uncover the importance of reputation in international negotiations. A leader needs to follow policies consistently in order to allow others to determine whether maintenance of the regime is in their interests. A leader also needs to ensure the continued support of junior partners by adhering to promises. A leader with a reputation of consistency is more likely to maintain a winning coalition than is one with a reputation for either inconsistency or treachery.

Reputations may represent genuine private desires on the part of statesmen, or they may be a form of self-conscious policy 'branding' on their part. Such 'brands' may be policy packages that are consistently promoted as part of the statesman's stock-in-trade and in this way can become reputational resources that a politician would be loathe to compromise by making dramatic shifts in policy position. Either way, the statesman becomes associated over time with a relatively well-articulated policy position, from which it is costly to deviate in office (Laver 1997, 136).

## 3.5 The Problem of Decision-Making Structure

Despite conventions referring to states or corporations 'acting' as if they were unitary rational actors akin to single rational individual human beings, no matter how much we talk about 'Russia' dong this, or 'Microsoft' doing that, the fact is that all of these large negotiating entities are composed of much more complex decision-making structures. Robert Putnam first articulated the theory that international agreements are the product of negotiations at both the internal domestic and external international level – a 'two level game' (1988).[2] Likewise Graham Allison's second model of decision-making, the 'organisational process model,' depicts policy as the product of 'large semi-feudal, loosely allied organizations' (1971, 67). The implications of these models are discussed below.

### *3.5.1 Two-level Games*

While the 'one-level' games we have considered above focus on the single unitary rational actor and its interaction with other single unitary rational actios, the two-level game focuses on the role of this actor as a 'gate-keeper' between international negotiation games and donestic negotiation games. Crucially, the gate-keeper often needs internal ratification for externally negotiated agreements. This may come in the form of political ratification of international agreements, or ratification by shareholders or boards of directors for a takeover, merger, or expansion into a new market.

Two-level games occur simultaneously, as key decision-makers try to reach agreement with their international counterparts while at the same time trying to get these agreements accepted by their domestic constituencies. Thus a simple rational calculation of costs and benefits in the international game will not suffice as decision-makers are subject to internal pushes and pulls that may weight policy in what would appear to international observers to be an irrational direction.

For example the decision made by Margaret Thatcher, the Prime Minister of the United Kingdom at the time, to send a task force to recapture the Falkland (Malvinas) Islands that had been seized by Argentinean forces was unexpected by Argentina's military junta, as in cost-benefit terms the material value of the islands was minimal.

---

[2] Chapter three further develops the concept of two level games with reference to the role of the international negotiator.

What the Junta had not counted on was that Thatcher was an unpopular nationalist politician facing reelection. She was particularly susceptible to the pushes and pulls of internal public opinion with regard to defense of UK sovereign territory.

Two-level games focus on 'win-sets' defined as the set of all possible Level I (international) agreements that would 'win' or gain the necessary majority among the internal Level II internal domestic constituencies (Putnam 1988, 439). Putnam hypothesized that larger win-sets make Level I agreement more likely and, conversely, the smaller the win-set the more likely the negotiations will break down. However, the difficulty of gaining internal ratification can also be used as a strategic bargaining chip in Level I international negotiations in an attempt to gain further concessions through 'salami' (just one more slice for the folks back home) tactics.

Thus we cannot categorically state what the nature of the impact of the win-set might be upon Level I negotiations, but it is often likely to be considerable, even to the extent of denying a potential Pareto optimal solution to the international game, or altering the dominant strategies of decision-makers. Essentially the logic of two-level games requires us to look at the vertical interaction the constitutive elements of a larger decision-making entity. However, Allison's organizational process model directs us to also consider horizontal components of the decision-making structure to which we will now turn.

### *3.5.2 The Organizational Process Model*

For Allison, the simplification of Model 1 (RAM) should not be allowed to conceal the fact that governments (and potentially other large entities such as multi-national organizations) consist of a 'conglomerate of semi-feudal, loosely allied organizations, each with a substantial life of its own' (1971, 67). The organizational process model, or Model 2, depicts international negotiation policy as the product of interaction between these entities.

The interplay between different elements of the decision-making bureaucracy helps explain how the larger decision-making entity (such as a state) could simultaneously be pursuing apparently irrational or even mutually contradictory policy initiatives. Thus during the 'War on Drugs' pursued by the Reagan Administration of the United States in the late 1980s, the Central Intelligence Agency (CIA) and senior elements of the U.S. administration were actively involved in the trafficking of drugs in order to help fund clandestine military operations in support of the 'Contra' guerillas fighting against the Sandinista regime of Nicaragua.

This model proposes that 'quasi-independent actors' address policy issues, and that each organization or department in the larger policy decision-making process works within a set of decision-making tools and routines known as standard operating procedures (SOPs). SOPs deal with foreign policy issues as a logical response to problems that occur on a regular basis. Foreign policy decision-making then resembles an assembly line whereby routine problems are dealt with by applying prefabricated solutions.

Allison uses Simon's concept of satisficing (adopting the first policy that seems adequately to fit needs – a combination of satisfy and suffice) to give an indication of the reasons for choosing a slightly inappropriate policy rather than searching for perfect solutions. The construction of SOPs itself imposes costs, thus organizations find any needle in the haystack rather than searching for the sharpest (Allison 1971, 71-72). Connected with this is the concept of using tried and tested policies rather than looking for new ones. This means that optimal strategies may not be pursued because the costs of uncovering them is seen to outweigh the benefit to be had over and above those that merely 'satisfice.'

## 3.6 The Impact of the Individual

### *3.6.1 Irrationality*

Allison presents the bureaucratic politics model, or Model 3, as a second alternative to the rational actor model. In this model bureaucrats and governmental players bargain with each other to define what is the national interest and the best way for the national interest to be fulfilled. This model could equally well be applied to department heads in a multinational corporation.

The bureaucratic politics model contains a number of key factors and criteria. First, as with Model 2, governments are not seen as unitary actors. However, rather than decision-making being viewed from the perspective of semi-feudal, loosely allied organizations, Model 3 instead considers the individuals at the head of each of these organizations and departments; sets of players that hold policy-making positions.

Second, these players hold a diverse set of interests, which they hope to pursue and translate into policy. Consequently, different players maintain different policy preferences on the same issue. The motivations for individual players are shaped by triple-tiered hierarchies of preferences; by their own conceptions of what is the public good or the national interest, by their own organizational affiliation and its needs and interests, and by personal interests and career ambitions.

Third, policy-making players interact with each other along regularized circuits of the policy process, or in regular political games, and they work to ensure that their preferences are met with personally positive outcomes. Thus, foreign policy decisions are the result of negotiations among skilled policy-making practitioners and the outcome of internal political machinations. Allison writes: 'to explain why a particular formal governmental decision was made, or why one pattern of governmental behavior emerged, it is necessary to identify the games and players, to display the coalitions, bargains and compromises, and to convey some feel for the confusion' (1971, 146).

The problem with individuals having such influence upon international negotiation is that we can presume neither that individual human beings *will* always act in a rational manner, nor that they will act in a uniform, standardized form of rationality in the real world. An individual may well not receive the information (in terms of either quantity or quality) needed to fulfill the conditions of rational choice. Alternatively, it might be a question of information overload, and an inadequate system for sorting, prioritizing or discarding. Time pressure (which is particularly in evidence during periods of crisis) may well undermine any attempt at a reasonable evaluation of the facts and available options.

If we were to try truly to analyze an individual's decision-making priorities, we would have to have a fairly deep knowledge of that individual's psychological profile. For instance, in an experiment conducted in 1962 by Hermann and Hermann, it was found that groups of actors with psychological profiles matched to those of the major decision-makers in 1914 commenced hostilities, when placed in a role-play simulation of the events leading up to the First World War. However, control groups of non-matched individuals called a conference and reached a negotiated settlement (Stoessinger 1990, 130).

Sidney Verba has in fact drawn up a list of six different variables through which irrationality may enter the model via the medium of the individual, and concludes that:

> The international system becomes the arena into which unresolved personal problems are projected. Evidence from the clinical studies of individuals as well as from correlation studies of larger groups suggests that there is indeed a relationship between personality variables and early childhood experiences, on the one hand, and attitudes on a wide range of topics, including international relations on the other (1969, 219 and 221-222).

However, although 'it is a truism that all action within the international system can be reduced to the actions of individuals,' this does not necessarily mean that it is always a good thing in terms of foreign policy analysis to do so (Snyder 1962, 41). We may conclude that individuals matter, but the question remains, do they matter enough for the added level of analytical complexity to be justified by the increase in explanatory power, or will a different unit of analysis suit our purposes better?

### *3.6.2 Perceptions*

Further difficulties emerge when we consider the different perception filters through which actors view the world, and which have considerable bearing not only upon how they reach their 'rational' decisions, but even upon the processing of information upon which they will construct their preference hierarchies. Perceptions are unique to every individual, being based not only on shared experiences and images, but also upon personal ones, as well as history, culture, and the biological and psychological make-up of the specific actors concerned. Perception affects decision-making rationality through self-imaging and what has become known as 'perception of the other.'

Consistency in foreign policy can therefore be seen as a result, not of the irrelevance of individuals, but in terms of the strong tendency for people to see what they expect to see and to assimilate incoming information to fit pre-existing images formed through national, organizational and personal experience, through planning and by virtue of those factors foremost in the decision-maker's mind when an incident occurs (Jervis 1976, 117).

> The evidence from both psychology and history overwhelmingly supports the view…that decision-makers tend to fit incoming information into their existing theories and images. Indeed, their theories and images play a large part in determining what they notice. In other words actors tend to perceive what they expect (Jervis 1969, 240).

Simon's concept of satisficing (adopting the first policy that seems to adequately fit the information) that Allison uses in relation to his bureaucratic model can also be applied to perceptions. People tend to adopt the first image of their adversary that seems to fit his actions, and are very reluctant to subsequently change this perception. This may not be an instinctive 'first impression,' but may be the result of a 'rational' decision. If the actor believes that his first, tentative guesses will soon be corrected if they are wrong and can be of assistance if they are right, he will not hesitate to make them.

Unfortunately, the assumption that wrong guesses will soon be rectified is erroneous. Actors will continue a fair way down a blind alley before they realize that their basic assumption needs revision. This is due to the fact that they will 'ignore information that does not fit, twist it so that it confirms, or at least does not contradict their beliefs, and deny its validity – Confirming evidence, by contrast, is quickly and accurately noted' (Jervis 1976, 143).

Robin Cook, former British Foreign Secretary, accused allied leaders of precisely this sort of thought process in the lead up to and during the Second Gulf War. It was assumed that Saddam Hussein was an evil dictator who possessed weapons of mass destruction, was not afraid to use them, and would be willing to pass them on to others. Any evidence that seemed to confirm these suspicions was rapidly assimilated. Any evidence that seemed to refute the claims was rejected, ignored, or used to demonstrate how clever Hussein was at hiding the weapons, and thus he was deemed to be even guiltier due to the obvious premeditation of his acts. Any processes that held out hope for clarification of the issue, if they looked like producing negative confirmation, were likewise curtailed (Tempest, 2003).

A number of general points can be made with regard to the impact of prejudicial, stereotypical, biased, or 'partisan' perceptions upon decision-making in international negotiations. First, it is likely that the more uncertainty that surrounds the information upon which decision-makers are formulating policy, the greater the impact of pre-existing theories and images upon interpretation of the data. If messages are sent from a different background of concerns and information than is possessed by the receiver, misunderstanding is more likely due to cultural, political, social, linguistic, historical, and cognitive dissonance.

Second, the surer a decision-maker is about the validity of their pre-existing theories and images, the greater the impact upon interpretation of the data. Third, the more effort has been expended by the decision-maker in the construction of their pre-existing theories and images, the more likely they are to be entrapped by these 'sunk costs,' and therefore the more resistant they are likely to be to new ideas or images.

As a result of partisan perceptions, actors tend to overlook the fact that evidence consistent with their theories may also be consistent with other views or explanations for the actions of others. They also tend to overlook the fact that more than one interpretation or explanation can be placed upon their own actions. Actors tend to see others as more hostile than they are, and to interpret the signals of others in a more negative way than they were likely intended.

We are familiar in all forms of international negotiation with the tendency towards 'worst case' analysis, where it is considered rational to assume and prepare for the worst. If the effect of another's action is to injure or threaten the actor, he is apt to believe that such was the other's purpose and intent. On the other hand, actors tend to see their own actions and signals in the best possible light and are confused or hurt when others do not share this perception.

Ironically, actors often perceive their negotiating partners as more rational than they actually are. While actors are often very aware of their own internal political games, nevertheless, there remains a tendency to perceive the behavior of others (especially in the international environment) as more centralized, disciplined, and coordinated, and therefore more rational (in unitary rational actor terms) than is actually the case. Because a state gets most of its information about the other state's policies from the other's foreign office, it tends to take the foreign office's position for the stand of the government as a whole.

Likewise the statements of chairmen and chief executive officers are often perhaps given undue weight. Thus when in 1991, Gerald Ratner, the son of the founder of the successful British chain of retailers, Ratners Jewellery, said in a speech at the Institute of Directors that some of their products were 'total crap' and others cost less than a prawn sandwich but would not last as long, the previously thriving company suffered huge losses.

## 3.7 Dealing with Individual Rationality and Perceptions

The first step towards dealing with the problems presented by individuals in international negotiation is to assess who is able to have an impact upon a particular negotiation, what that impact is likely to be, and to what degree their individual personalities, prejudices and characteristics can be brought to bear. Initially then, it often makes sense to draw up a 'relationship map' within which patterns of influence, deference, and antagonism are mapped. This can then be combined with a model of the decision-making structure within which they find themselves in order to assess the extent of individual input, and also the impact of others upon the decision-maker.

### *3.7.1 Relationship Mapping*

The Harvard Negotiation Project and the Conflict Management Group under the leadership of Roger Fisher have conducted both a great deal of research and a large number of practical workshops on this process. This section will draw upon some of the insights gained by the authors when attending a certification training program in Cambridge.

The process of relationship mapping requires decision-makers and analysts to:

1. Clarify and prioritize *your own interests*;
2. Identify and map all relevant *players*;
3. Identify all *players' key interests*;

4. Identify and characterize *relationships* among the players;
5. Plan and implement a *sequence of one-on-one negotiations* to leverage and/or reshape the relationship map to serve your interests - short-and long term.

1. It is important to realize that an individual's interests are not necessarily the same as the positions they take (Fisher et al 1991, 40-55). Positions are an individuals' demands, or list of wants. Underlying these positions are the reasons parties demand something: their needs, concerns, desires, hopes and fears. A negotiated agreement that satisfies the interests of all parties has a good chance of lasting success, and is also achievable, even when parties take apparently irreconcilable positions. Understanding what your many interests may be will help establish what you really want from a negotiation, and may help you get what you need.

   For instance, I want a pay raise from my employer. My boss is adamant however that there is no money to give me such a raise even though she is very sympathetic to my request, wants to retain my services, and of course firmly believes I fully deserve more recognition. If I go into the meeting demanding more money, it is likely that negotiations will break down, and I will then be in a no-win situation – either I back down and lose face, or I walk out from my job and join the ranks of the unemployed.

   If however I first ask myself, why do I need more money? The answer may be that my interests lie in getting a new apartment. Coincidentally, my employers have some properties that are not currently occupied, and which they might be willing to lease to me either for free (constituting a pay rise) or for the amount I am currently paying (constituting a fulfillment of my interests at no extra costs). By clarifying and prioritizing my interests, I turn a zero-sum negotiation in which I am most likely to lose out, into a solution which leaves everybody happy. So in constructing a hierarchy of preferred outcomes, we need to consider how each outcome relates to our hierarchy of interests in the short, medium, and long-term.

2. The next step requires listing all relevant players, including all those who are influenced or affected by the outcome of the negotiation or its implementation, as well as those who can influence or affect the outcome or implementation. Although some individuals or groups may appear powerless, it may nevertheless make sense to take the interests of all into account in order to ensure a lasting settlement. Likewise, although there is a temptation in negotiations to deal only with moderates who are more likely to reach agreement, a truly sustainable settlement requires that extremists' interests are addressed.

   The relevancy of an organization or individual is measured subjectively by the party doing the mapping. Strategic mapping requires not only the clarification of one's own interests, but also the identification of all who could affect the fulfillment of these aspirations in either a positive or negative way. It makes sense therefore, once all the major players or stake-holders have been identified, to create a diagram outlining all stake-holding groups, the individuals within them, other independent stakeholders and, finally, where you sit among those stakeholders. More detailed modeling of the decision-making of stake-holders and the influence of other players is carried out in the following section.

3. Once all the players have been mapped, it is then important to

clarify and map their interests in order to identify those that conflict with or complement your own. Here it is also vital to be aware of our own unsubstantiated assumptions about the values and interests of others. In particular we need to beware of cultural stereotypes and generalizations (including social, economic, political, religious, etc.), and the influence such prejudices have upon our assumptions. Section 7.3.3 addresses these problems in detail and also suggests ways for overcoming them.

4. Once all the players and their interests have been mapped, it is possible to look at interests that conflict with or complement each other. It then becomes necessary to map the kinds of relationships between various parties in order to identify potential leverage situations. Fisher et al break these types of relationships down into three broad groups: deference, influence or antagonism.

   Deference exists when Party A will almost certainly do what party B does or will do what Party B asks, advises or directs them to do. Deference can emerge as a result of power, seniority, expertise, status, reputation, mentorship, sponsorship, personal respect or admiration. Under influence, Party A is likely to follow Part B's lead, or do what party B advises, asks or directs them to do. Influence can come about through a successful track record, shared interests, trust of judgment or best intentions. Antagonism means that Party A will not follow Party B's lead, do what they advise, ask or directs, and in fact is likely to pull in precisely the opposite direction. Antagonism can result from previous interactions, conflicting interests, or partisan perceptions. The nature of these relationships should also then be plotted onto the relationship map.

5. Finally, it is necessary to identify groups of players with shared or complimentary interests with whom you might reach mutually beneficial arrangements or alliances, and also those who might undermine your interests, and who might lean on others to produce an alliance antagonistic to your interests. Looking at your relationship map it then becomes possible to plan a sequence of negotiations to build a winning coalition in favor of your interests.

   Strategically this can take the form of 'bootstrapping' from easier parties to 'harder' ones, 'backward mapping' from needed decision-makers to yourself, 'pyramiding' from 'hardest' and most 'impactful' downward to other parties and/or sequencing to conceal or reveal information. All of these strategic negotiating ploys rely upon the exploitation of patterns of deference, influence and antagonism.

Relationship mapping can be seen as something of a macro overview of the parties with whom you are carrying out international negotiations. However, given problems of decision-making structure and the impact of the individual mentioned above, it is clear that in some instances we will need to delve into a much more detailed micro analysis. More complex decision-making modeling as an attempt to further clarify the role played by individual decision-makers, and also the influence of others upon them, is addressed in the following section.

### *3.7.2 Decision-Making Modeling Process*

Allison's models may be combined in a single decision-making model through the inclusion of structure, role and personality filters within the black box of decision-making. However, we also need to incorporate the impact of other actors upon the decision-maker through analysis of the various operating environments from which feedback is obtained. For Karl Deutsch, the feedback process is at the heart of all effective goal-seeking behavior and refers to the sending back to the acting system of a steam of information about the results of its own earlier actions (1978).

The system thus gets information about the results of what it has just done, and uses this information to modify its subsequent action. Positive feedback always increases the intensity or frequency of original behavior whereas negative feedback serves to reduce or reverse previous behavior (Deutsch 1978, 92-93). Deutsch refers to a simple cascade model of national decision making consisting of five levels, each a distinct reservoir of public or elite opinion and each reservoir linked to a particular complex of social institutions and status groups.

The first of these is the social and economic elite, which does not form a simple monolithic group, but rather is connected by a dense net of multiple ties, links, and channels of communication. The second is the political and governmental elite, which is also not monolithic. Third we have the media of mass communication, fourth the network of local opinion leaders, and fifth the politically relevant strata of the population at large. Streams of information move downward in cascade fashion, from higher-level communications systems to lower-level ones.

> Each of the five groups, however, has its own memories and its own measure of autonomy. Each can reject, ignore, or reinterpret many – perhaps almost all – unpalatable messages. Each is capable of innovation and initiative. And each can also feed back a stream of information upward to some or all of the higher-level groups (Deutsch 119-122).

## <Figure 3.2> The Cybernetic Model of Policy Formulation

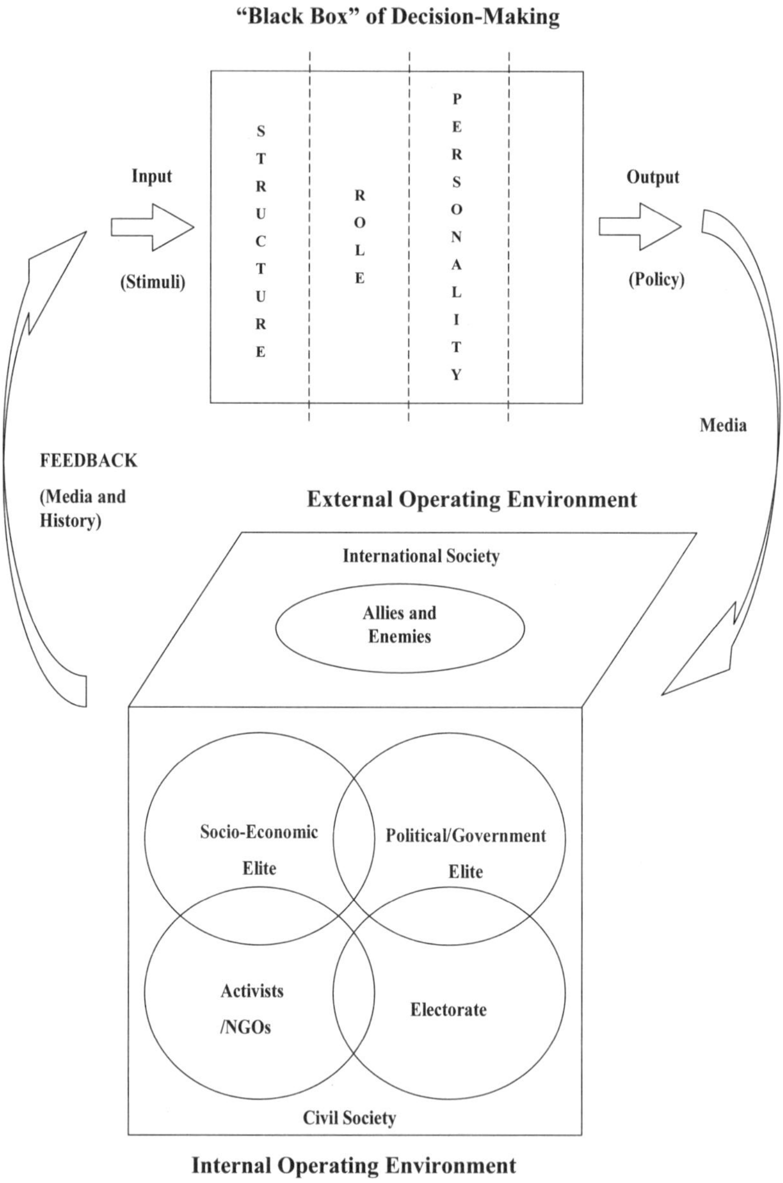

When combined with the external operating environment examined in the relationship mapping exercise above, these streams of information help explain why leaders might feel the need to act in ways contrary to those dictated by a simple cost-benefit analysis of their positions. David Allen notes that the external environment of any one state in the system 'fundamentally encompasses all the other states in the system, both individually and in a variety of combinations' (1989).

Figure 3.2 (above) presents a graphical representation of this more complex model of decision-making in the international security environment. It incorporates elements of Graham Allison's decision-making models within three filters, and also Deutsch's simple cascade model and his analysis of five levels of societal influence upon decision-making through the civil society operating environment and elements of the feedback loop. In addition it contains elements of the external operating environment contained in our previous discussion of relationship mapping.

### *3.7.3 Dealing with Perceptional Challenges*

Having identified possible reasons for individual decision-makers in international negotiations acting in apparently irrational ways, acting according to a different rationality from that expected, or in accordance with different perceptions of the nature of the negotiation, we now turn to strategies for overcoming these limitations. First and foremost, most simply put, we need to try to look at the negotiation or conflict from the other person's perspective. This does not mean that we will ultimately agree with their position, but it does mean that we should make every effort to understand it. We are trying to comprehend rather than to 'buy into' their reasoning by placing ourselves in their shoes, or in their seat, and thereby gain an insight into their mind-set.

This process can actually be extremely beneficial to our own position. The more we learn about others' concerns, the more likely we are to consider elements that had previously escaped our notice, the more likely we are to change our own minds and the more likely we are to revise our thinking. Rethinking our policy may well be a benefit rather than a cost of understanding an adversary's point of view. With greater knowledge we might reduce the area of conflict and increase the chance of advancing our newly enlightened self-interest. We might also discard policies that are doomed to fail or encounter such resistance from the other that they become irrational (although we did not know this to be the case before we increased our strategic comprehension) before becoming entrapped through sunk costs.

Theorists such as Roger Fisher (1991; 1997) and John Burton (1969; 1990a; 1990b) have tried to formalize and model this process. The first step is to assess our own assumptions about the negotiation or conflict, and the data upon which we base them (sometimes called Assessing the First Position). Next, it is important to Assess the Second Position - consider what the other parties see (their partisan perceptions), why they see it that way (their background, emotions and motives), and what underlies their positions (interests) (Fisher et al 1997, 48-51).

Both of these forms of assessment are carried out through a process of 'cognitive mapping.' We address our cognitive maps and infer those of other parties by studying assertions and causal beliefs. Why do we perceive the actions of others in a particular way, and, given our understanding of what they believe, or state they believe, how are they likely to perceive these actions of ours? This has been modeled by the Assumptions/Data Tool shown below.

**<Figure 3.3> The Assumptions/Data Tool (Fisher et al 1997, 49)**

| **A. Assumptions**<br>*What are my core assumptions about the conflict?* | **B. Base Data**<br>*On what data do I base my assumptions?* |
|---|---|
| **D. Alternative Assumptions**<br>*Taking the additional data into account, what might be some alternative conclusions about the conflict?* | **C. Nonconforming Data**<br>*What additional data might be taken into account that may be inconsistent with my core assumptions?* |

The third step is to interact with the other parties in order to test our understanding of their positions. For Fisher and his associates this has tended to take the form of role-play workshops through which parties are engaged directly or indirectly in communication. For followers of John Burton, the process has tended to involve a problem-solving workshop within which each party must explain the other's position to the satisfaction of the other (1969).

Finally, given this new understanding, instead of focusing on how to achieve our own goals, in the interests of a more lasting settlement and maintenance of a long-term cooperative relationship, we consider whether there are other ways in which we can ensure the substantive interests of the other party. This was the basis of the historic 'land for peace' approach to the conflict between the Israelis and Palestinians (and other Arab nations) that has come closer than any other process to ensuring peace in the Middle East.

Traditional approaches to ensuring national security in a hostile environment such as the international anarchic environment have focused on maximizing military strength in order to deter attack from others. Unfortunately such a policy of 'self-help' has often led to increased insecurity, as other actors perceive even defensive weapons as a threat to their own national security, resulting in arms racing and hostile posturing (the security dilemma).

Land for peace is a revolutionary approach aimed instead at

fulfilling some of the desires of those that oppose you, thereby reducing the hostility and level of threat they in turn pose to you. In the particular context of the Arab-Israeli conflict, Israel was encouraged to relinquish control of all or part of the Arab territories it conquered, and begin a process that would result in the eventual construction of a Palestinian homeland in return for peace with and recognition by the Arab world.

The formula appeared for the first time in UN Security Council Resolution 242 in 1967 in the aftermath of the Six Day War and was first used as the basis for Israel's peace treaty with Egypt in 1979. The principle reappeared in the Oslo Accords between Israel and representatives of the Palestinian Liberation Organization (PLO), which were finalized in Oslo, Norway on August 20, 1993 and subsequently officially signed at a public ceremony in Washington D.C. on September 13, 1993, according to which the Israelis would hand over most of the territotries they had formerly occupied, which were to form the foundations of a future Palestinian state. In return relations were to be normalised, and terrorist attacks upon Israel were to cease.

Although, as is clear from the continuation of hostilities which have recently (July 2006) escalated to include a re-invasion of Lebanon by Israel, the process has been far from complete, any failure has in all probability been due to the lack of recognition of the decision-making complexities of the parties involved rather than limitations of the Assumption/Data Tool, the problem solving workshop, or the basic formula of land for Peace. This brings us to the final consideration of practical dilemmas in international negotiations, the impact of crisis considerations upon decision-making.

## 3.8 Crisis Decision-Making in International Negotiations

A crisis situation occurs when there is a perceived serious threat to high priority goals, when the amount of time allowed for decision is sharply limited, and where the precipitating events have been unanticipated. The consequences of crisis environments include an increased occurrence of information overload or insufficiency, or at the very least increased ambiguity of data leading to the greater impact of pre-existing theories and images upon interpretation of the data. Fear of panic associated with crises can lead to increased threat perception and a greater tendency to perceive others in a negative light.

A sense of urgency can convey the message that there is insufficient time to engage in the kind of comprehensive analysis suggested by Fisher et al, and a greater tendency to look quickly for any needle in the haystack (satisficing) in terms of both perception formulation and policy applications, leading to rushed first impressions and decisions. In addition, the stress associated with crisis decision-making can lead to an increased rate of error, a tendency to aggression, a diminished focus of attention, highly selective perceptions, a failure to distinguish between sense and nonsense, a loss of ability to abstract, an increased tendency towards the personification of the problem, and general paranoia.

At the same time, under such circumstances, it is usual for a small group of individuals to form an isolated decision-making unit. The first consequence of this process is that there is less chance individual eccentricities will be cancelled out by a larger rational consensus. Secondly, there is more chance of information overload, as there are fewer individuals to deal with input. Thirdly, there is a danger of groupthink setting in. This is a process whereby the perceptions (or misperceptions) of the group are reinforced by their increased contact with each other and isolation from other perceptional inputs. Thus, 'the more intense the interaction between the parties, the more important it is to incorporate perceptional data into the analysis' (Holsti 1991, 158).

In addition to the need to be ever more aware of decision-making structures and perceptional input during crisis moments, both Fisher and Burton advise us to deconstruct the nature of the conflict itself and the identity of the participants. Fisher advocates that we 'separate the people from the problem' in order to reduce hostility and encourage the notion of negotiators as joint problem-solvers rather than opponents (1991, 17). Meanwhile, it is also important to keep in mind Burton's conclusion that people most commonly come into conflict because they feel that their identity is not being recognized, that they are not being treated with dignity and respect due them as individual human beings and the bearers of rights and needs (1990b); even when the conflict appears to be about something much more material such as land or resources.

## 3.9 Conclusion

In this chapter we have identified a number of problems facing us, and the practitioners of international negotiations when we try to implement some of the theoretical models from Chapter 2. In particular, problems associated with the multilateral nature of international negotiations, the structure of international negotiations decision-making, the rationality and perceptions of individuals (particularly in cross-cultural negotiations) and crisis decision-making have demonstrated how far practice can at times seem to stray from theory.

However, we have also briefly examined the ongoing work of

theorists in attempting to address these problems, and also the spillover of such ideas into the 'real world' of conflict resolution and prevention. In the following chapters we will examine further instances of international negotiations in practice, paying particular attention to the roles of individuals as negotiators, facilitators, mediators, and advocates, and some of the strategic and tactical methods they employ in order to achieve the results they desire and build mutually beneficial relationships.

## References

Allen, David. 1989. 'The Context of Foreign Policy Systems: The Contemporary International Environment' in Michael Clarke and Brian White (eds.) *Understanding Foreign Policy: The Foreign Policy Systems Approach.* Aldershot: Edward Elgar, pp 60-83.

Allison, Graham. 1971. *Essence of Decision.* Boston: Little, Brown and Company.

Burton, John W. 1969. *Conflict and Communication.* London: Macmillan.

Burton, John W. 1990a. *Conflict: Resolution and Prevention.* New York: St Martins Press.

Burton, John W. 1990b. *Conflict: Human Needs Theory* New York: St Martins Press.

Deutsch, Karl W. 1978. *The Analysis of international relations, 2e.* New Jersey: Prentice-Hall.

Fisher, Roger, William Ury and Bruce Patton. 1991. *Getting to Yes.* New York: Penguin.

Fisher, Roger, Andrea Kupfer Schneider, Elizabeth Bogwardt & Brian Ganson. 1997. *Coping with International Conflict.* New

Jersey: Prentice-Hall.

Harding, Garrett. 1968. 'Tragedy of the Commons' *Science* 13 December 1968: Vol. 162. no. 3859, pp. 1243 – 1248.

Holsti, K.J. 1991. *Peace and War: Armed Conflicts and International Order 1648-1989.* Cambridge: Cambridge University Press.

Howe, Brendan. 2006. 'Rationality and Intervention in an Anarchic Society' *Korean Journal of Defense Analysis* Vol. 18, No. 1 (Spring 2006) pp 161-185.

Jervis, Robert. 1969. 'Hypothesis on Misperception' in *International Politics and Foreign Policy: A Reader in Research and Theory*, ed. James Rosenau. New York: The Free Press.

Jervis, Robert. 1976. *Perception and Misperceptions in International Politics,* Princeton, NJ: Princeton University Press.

Laver, Michael. 1997. *Private Desires, Political Action: An Invitation to the Politics of Rational Choice*. London: Sage.

Putnam, Robert D. 1988. 'Diplomacy and Domestic Politics: The Logic of Two-Level Games.' *International Organization*, Vol. 42, No. 3 (Summer, 1988), pp. 427-460.

Snyder, R.C. H.W. Bruck and B. Sapin (eds.) 1962. *Foreign Policy Decision-Making,* New York: Free Press.

Stoessinger, John. 1990. *Why Nations go to War (5e).* New York: St Martin's Press.

Tempest, Matthew. 2003. 'Cook Doubts Saddam Threat.' *The Guardian* (June 17)

Verba, Sidney. 1969. 'Assumptions of Rationality and Non-Rationality in Models of the International System,' in *International Politics and Foreign Policy: A Reader in Research and Theory*, ed. James Rosenau. New York: The Free Press, pp. 221-222.

# Chapter 4 The International Negotiator

## 4.1 Introduction

Any serious study of negotiations should deal with the role played by the negotiator. Without a negotiator, negotiations cannot take place. Despite this obvious fact, it is interesting to observe that most books about negotiations are silent about the negotiator. They presume that negotiators are rational-decision makers, meaning that they try to maximize pay-offs. This fails to do justice to the complexity of the negotiator's role in the international setting, since international negotiators face rather stringent constraints. In this chapter, we explore these constraints in detail, highlighting the two-level aspect of international negotiations. At one level, international interface occurs between negotiators; at another level, domestic interface occurs between the negotiator and her local constituency.

The two-level nature of international negotiations offers a very useful perspective on the role of the international negotiator. These two levels – international level and domestic level – interact with each other through the process of negotiations. Any international negotiator finds her role to be all of advocate, coordinator and facilitator. We will take an in-depth look at these roles.

## 4.2 Two-levels of International Negotiation

International negotiations are two-level games. At one level, the negotiator from one country (or one multinational organization) meets her negotiating counterpart from the other country (or another multinational organization). Here she explains her country's interests to her counterpart, listens to her counterpart's interests, and tries to get the most she can for her country. This interface among international negotiators is what we call "Level I". Commonly, this Level I is what is referred to as "international negotiations". Level I defines only one level of international negotiations, however. There is another level of the game, where all domestic stakeholders try to have their interests reflected in the negotiations. This interface among domestic stakeholders is what we call "Level II".

**<Figure 4.1> The Two-Level Game of International Negotiations**

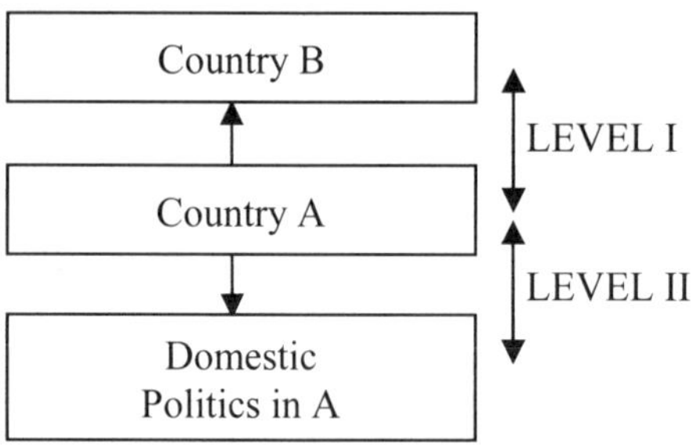


An international negotiator does not present her own view to her counterpart at the bargaining table. No country or international organization gives complete discretion to its negotiator. When an international negotiator meets her counterpart, what she can negotiate with her counterpart is predetermined by her country's domestic politics.

An international negotiator can agree to her counterpart's proposal at Level I, if and only if such an agreement is acceptable to her domestic political constituents. An agreement at Level I is not going to be politically viable if it fails to secure political legitimacy at home. In a typical representative democracy, an international agreement goes through the domestic approval process thorough the parliament/legislative branch. This process is called the ratification process. An agreement which fails to be ratified domestically is an agreement in form only, and not operative nationally. It is merely a document and not an effective agreement. The very purpose of an agreement goes beyond documentation of mutual terms and condition of resolving dispute among the parties, to effectively reflecting a "meeting of the minds" or intent of the parties to fulfill those terms, and then to ensuring the enforcement of the agreement. Hence, any international negotiator should take the issue of ratification seriously.

### *4.2.1 Winsets*

The set of all possible Level I (international) agreements that would successfully receive ratification at Level II (domestic) is called the 'win-set' (Putnam 1988). International negotiators play their game within the boundaries of the win-set.

**<Figure 4.2> Win-set**

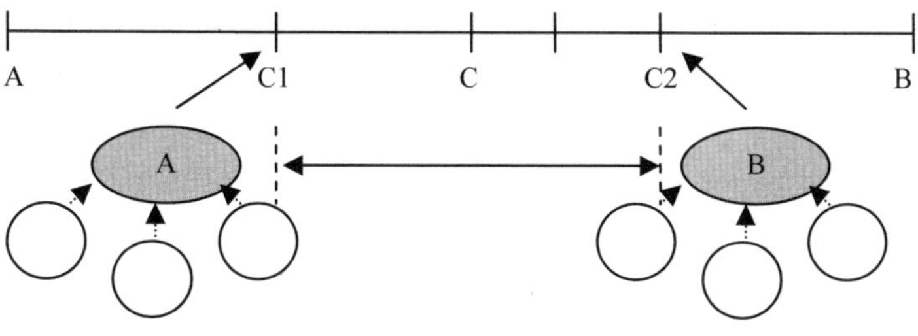

The concept of the win-set can be illustrated by a diagram. Suppose country A and country B are negotiating with each other. Within each country, various stakeholders are trying to influence its representative. Through this domestic process, the win-set of each country emerges. In Figure 2, the line segment AB represents the maximum joint gain from the negotiations between country A and B. That is, the entire line length of AB represents the gain to be divided by country A and B. In the diagram, point A is the lowest gain for country A. As it moves further from A, the share of gains for country A becomes larger. Point B is the lowest gain for country B. As it moves further from B, the share of gains for country B becomes larger. If they agree on the division of the gain at point C, then country A gets the segment AC, and country B gets the segment BC.

Now, suppose C1 is the point at the ratification in country A can be secured, and C2 is country B's ratification point. This means that the win-set for country A is the line segment BC1, and the win-set for country B is the line segment AC2. That is, country A can accept any agreement as long as the division of the gain is larger than AC1, while country B can accept any agreement as long as the division of the gain is larger than BC2. In this case, there is an overlapping area of the win-set of countries A and B, which is C1C2. This overlapping zone of the win-set of the negotiating parties is called as ZOPA (zone of the possible agreement).

The domestic process where this win-set is negotiated is Level II of international negotiations. Within this range of the win-set, a negotiator tries to find the best solution. Hence, it is a mistake to think that an international negotiator decides on her own what to agree with her counterpart at the negotiating table. What an international negotiator does is, to a large extent, shadowed by the win-set dictated by the domestic politics of her country – that is, Level II. An international negotiator's lips and hands are tied by

Level II: whatever occurs at Level I is predetermined by Level II.

In order to predict the outcome of the international negotiations, we need to look inside the domestic politics of the countries involved in the negotiations. To analyze this Level II negotiation, the concept of the win-set is in need of further elaboration.

### *4.2.2 How is the win-set determined?*

Conceptually, the win-set is determined thorough a series of negotiations in the domestic arena. Unlike international negotiations at Level I, where negotiators from each country convene at a specific venue, domestic negotiations at Level II do not take such a form: not every stakeholder negotiates at a single, visible venue. Rather, domestic negotiations at Level II are multi-layered, and the venue for the negotiations is not predetermined. It is likely that stakeholders with large stakes will find ways to access the relevant parties and to make their input into the Level II negotiations in visible or less transparent ways.

Prior to entering into international negotiations, it is typical to forge a domestic consensus among the key political players. The nature of negotiations *per se* determines the identity of the key player or key players. At intergovernmental negotiations, the Ministry of Foreign Affairs (the State Department in the case of the U.S.) does not necessarily take the active leading role. Usually the Ministry in charge of the negotiating issues is in the driver's seat.

For instance, at the recent multi-lateral negotiations on the UNESCO convention on cultural diversity during 2004-2005, the Ministry of Culture was supposed to take a lead role, whereas the Ministry of Foreign Affairs was expected to coordinate the country's negotiating stance with other countries, as usual. The interests of artists were presented to, and represented by, the Ministry of Culture.

Some politicians had stakes in the UNESCO negotiations. Their interests were reflected through the usual channel of the government-political party communications.

Allegedly, the Ministry of Culture was at odds with the Ministry of Foreign Affairs. The draft agreement, which was about to be voted on by the member governments of UNESCO, had a clause to the effect that any previous international trade agreement may be nullified if a member government finds it necessary to preserve cultural diversity. The Ministry of Culture was in favor of the draft agreement on the table (which reflected the strong lobby of the artists), while the Ministry of Foreign Affairs had reservations about the draft agreement. If internal conflict continued, then the Korean government would not have been able to develop a unified negotiating stance. This is precisely the problem to be addressed by the domestic political process.

Sometimes, predetermined decision-making processes become obsolete. In the case of the Cuban Missile Crisis in 1962, United States President Kennedy came up with the idea of an *ad hoc* committee comprised of some of his cabinet members and military personnel. This committee adopted the decision rule of consensus. Kennedy did not use any existing decision-making process, nor did he involve any Congress members in the *ad hoc* committee. As history records, the *ad hoc* committee suffered confrontation between hardliners (asking for an immediate, all-out attack on missile sites in Cuba) and a group of people seeking a diplomatic solution. With the time for decision approaching rapidly, the committee could not agree on a particular course of action. It was Kennedy himself who calculated the risk of the surgical strike on the missile, and opted for blockade. He then tried to convince committee members, U.S. politicians and citizens to accept his choice.

The domestic political process of determining the win-set is rather ambiguous. Stakeholders, including the various government agencies, politicians, businesses, consumers, civic organizations, and the media, voice their concerns and try to press their interests using various formal and informal mechanisms. What emerges from the influence-peddling activities of various stakeholders is the win-set.

### *4.2.3 Is the win-set mutable?*

Since the win-set is determined through domestic political processes, it is incorrect to argue that the win-set is inflexible. If, in the course of the international negotiations, a change occurs in the political coalition in a country, then the win-set may change. Suppose a new government takes power through an election. This change may give rise to a change of win-set. For instance, if the Democrats take the Presidency of the United States, the next U.S. administration may be more conciliatory to North Korea and give serious consideration to holding bilateral talks with the DPRK. South Korea's negotiating approach with North Korea has experienced a sea-change since the Kim Dae-jung administration, which initiated the "Sun-Shine Policy."

Leaving the election cycle aside, the political leadership may change the win-set. A prime example is the ratification of the NAFTA (North America Free Trade Agreement) in the U.S. In the fall of 1993, the Clinton administration overcame an unfavorable political climate and succeeded in securing the ratification of the United States Congress. The Clinton administration's strategy included an active public media campaign, political war targeting demagogues, and engagement with politicians who were against the ratification. It paid off. Without political will and political capital, it is impossible to change the win-set.

To some extent, the win-set reflects a political climate beyond a political election cycle. For instance, many Koreans tend to believe that Korean agriculture should be protected. Whether this belief is scientific or nonsense is not the issue. Unless political leaders have political will and political capital to invest in changing this sentiment, this part of the win-set is immutable.

Quite often, the difficulty of gaining internal ratification is used as a strategic bargaining chip in Level I international negotiations, in an attempt to gain further concessions. U.S. trade negotiators are masters of this tactic. "The U.S. Congress will not accept this idea", and "If you fail to agree on this, the U.S. Congress will retaliate" have become their mantras. The E.U. trade negotiators are also fond of using this tactic: "The French farmers will find the idea of reducing farm subsidies unacceptable. If you are so persistent upon reducing them, I can assure you that the angry European farmers will hijack this negotiation." The Korean trade negotiators are no exception: "The rice issue is extremely politically sensitive in Korea. If you keep insisting on the opening of the Korean rice market, you are asking for trouble."

## 4.3 The International Negotiator

The two levels of international negotiation offer a useful lens through which the role of the international negotiator is understood. From the perspective of the two-level game, an effective international negotiator is someone who plays actively three different roles: advocate, coordinator and facilitator. Advocacy is the primary task of a negotiator. In advancing her interests, she needs all the power of convincing logic and mastery of all the information related to the negotiations, including history of the cases, precedents, laws and regulations, and expert views on the subject.

As explained, an international negotiator's actions and positions are bounded by her win-set. Since any agreement should be ratified in order to become effective, an international negotiator is constantly aware of the win-set. As the negotiations proceed over time, the significance of the win-set looms larger. The negotiator assesses the win-set at an early stage in the negotiations. For her, negotiations provide an opportunity for her to advocate her country's interests. However, delivering domestic interests alone is insufficient for the negotiations to move forward: advocacy alone is not going to carry the negotiations to a resolution.

Rather than active talking, active listening is more important to success in the negotiations. Otherwise, how can one figure out the interests and the win-set of the counterparty? Without knowing each other's win-set, there is no way to assess how much room is available for the negotiations. Lack of knowledge of the other side's win-set due to the lack of active listening stands in the way of effective negotiations.

**<Figure 4.3> The International Negotiator Facing the Two-Level Game**

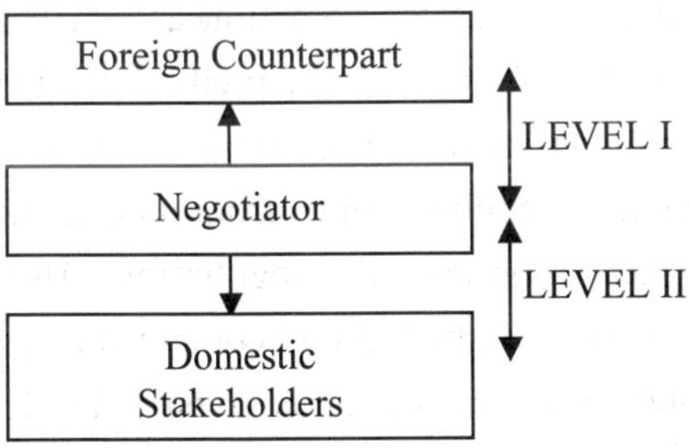


An effective international negotiator does not sit idle in the domestic process of forging political consensus at Level II. Rather, she works actively with stakeholders with a view to securing an advantageous negotiating position. For this purpose, she needs to communicate the negotiating counterpart's interests, concerns, preferences, and constraints to her domestic stakeholders. In this role, she is a coordinator. Effective communication to domestic stakeholders of the other country's interests, concerns, preferences, and constraints is instrumental in resolving a possible logjam of coordination among domestic government agencies, political parties, and civic organizations.

At the actual negotiations, the concept of the win-set takes the name of the 'mandate' to the negotiator. Mandates – usually understood as the negotiating guidelines in the international diplomatic community – reflect the win-set. For strategic purposes, it is often the case that the mandate given to the negotiator is narrower than the win-set. It is usually the case that the mandate is determined by the government prior to each round of the negotiations, and given to the negotiating team. This mandate binds the actions and words of the negotiator.

Sometimes, a mandate given to an international negotiator is just one instruction. In this case, the negotiator does not have any room for flexibility at the bargaining table. Sometimes, a mandate may offer the negotiator multiple options, with the predetermined order of preference among the options. In this case, the negotiator has some degree of flexibility. What her country wants from its negotiator is to achieve the most preferred option from the negotiations. However, if things are not going as well as wished, the negotiator may play with the less-preferred options. In this sense, she is given some flexibility. Probably, this scenario reflecting flexibility is closer to most international negotiating situations.

An effective international negotiator is someone who can use the two-level aspect of the negotiations to her strategic advantage. More often than not, talking to her negotiating counterpart at the negotiating table alone is not sufficient to deliver her message. Whenever negotiations enter a critical phase, or the negotiator confronts obstacles due to stubbornness in her counterpart, an international negotiator goes beyond the negotiating table. The press conference and the issue statement are the most common media for delivering messages to the domestic constituency of the other country.

The role of facilitator is rather unfamiliar territory for many international negotiators, who are used to the bilateral negotiation setting. Multilateral negotiations at the United Nations or the World Trade Organization require intellectual leadership; this is rarely the case in bilateral negotiations. For instance, when the parties to the General Agreement on Trade and Tariffs were negotiating for the creation of trading rules for services (at the Uruguay Round launched in 1986), they needed to come up with the very concept of "trade in services". Although some services such as banking and insurance were being internationally "traded," crafting a single, coherent framework for trade in services (applicable to all areas of services) was a daunting intellectual challenge. In order to move the negotiations forward, many countries, regardless of their commercial interests in the negotiations, contributed their ideas to the negotiators. Various written submissions and verbal proposals served as the starting point of the negotiations.

This activity of contributing one's intellectual ideas to the negotiations, (although the contribution is not directly linked to one's interests), describes the role of international negotiator as facilitator. Another example involves the Kyoto Protocol on Climate Change Convention in 1997, where the discussions went beyond agreeing to each country's greenhouse gas emissions reduction target. Recognizing the practical difficulty of enforcing each country's target either due to political concerns or business opposition, the

Kyoto protocol negotiators came up with the idea of 'emissions trading', where countries may meet their targets by purchasing greenhouse gas emission reductions from elsewhere. Of course, the Kyoto Protocol could have been completed without this interesting idea of emissions trading. However, the very inclusion of the emissions trading mechanims made the actual implementation of the goal of the global reduction of greenhouse gases more feasible.

## References

Byung-il Choi. 2005. 'Mad for Garlic: Domestic Politics of Trade Dispute' in *Korea and International Conflicts: Case Studies,* Volume 1, edited by Byung-il Choi, Institute for International Trade and Cooperation.

Putnam, Robert D. 1988. 'Diplomacy and Domestic Politics: The Logic of Two-Level Games.' *International Organization*, Vol. 42, No. 3 (Summer, 1988), pp. 427-460.

# Chapter 5 International Negotiations Process

## 5.1 Introduction

This chapter will take a closer look at the actual international negotiating scene, with a focus on the negotiations process. Practical knowledge about the negotiation process facilitates negotiations. A good negotiator can look forward what lies ahead in the negotiation process and take that into account in the current negotiating phase. This chapter begins with a general discussion of the international negotiations process: agenda setting - actual negotiations - agreement - ratification - implementation.

Quite often, there is a misunderstanding that the whole purpose of negotiations is to produce an agreement. The ultimate purpose of the negotiations is not merely to make a deal, but to ensure that the deal, if any, will be carried out. As it turns out, some agreements are not implemented as stated in the agreement. Why does this happen? How can the parties be protected in case of such an eventuality? These considerations lead to the discussion of dispute settlement, which is the second main topic of this chapter.

## 5.2 The General Process of International Negotiations

International negotiations move in phases. First of all, the parties to the negotiations (hereinafter "the parties") need to agree to negotiate. This sounds rather obvious. However, in reality, agreeing to negotiate is not that obvious and simple. International negotiations constitute explicit endeavors by the parties to address the on-going conflict through compromise, and not through other means such as war or unilateral sanction. Once the parties to a conflict agree to negotiate, they need to work on the agenda.

**<Figure 5.1> Phase of International Negotiations**

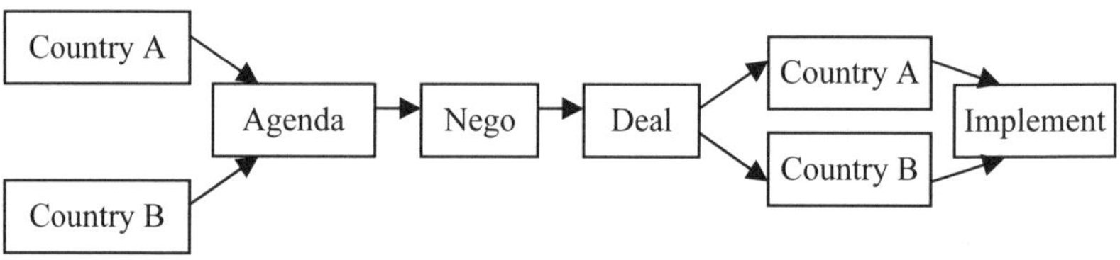


### *5.2.1 Agenda Setting*

The agenda includes the items for the negotiations, the time-frame for the negotiations and the negotiating modality. The items for the negotiations are the negotiating issues. The time-frame means the deadline for the negotiations and the meeting schedules. And the negotiating modality refers to the way the negotiations will be organized, and how they will be concluded.

For instance, the parties to the Uruguay Round, the last multilateral trade negotiations under the GATT, agreed on the following agenda when the Round was launched in 1986:

- Negotiating Issues:
  - Trade in goods:
    tariff reduction, agriculture, textile and clothing, antidumping, subsidies, and so on
  - Trade in services:
    establishment of the rules on trade in services, and trade liberalization in services
  - Trade aspects of intellectual property
  - Dispute settlement mechanism
- Time-frame:
  - Ministerial Meeting for the mid-term review in 1988, Montreal, Canada
  - Ministerial Meeting for concluding the round in 1990, Brussels, Belgium
- Modality:
  - Single-undertaking approach
  - Creation of 15 negotiating groups

At negotiations with many issues, some issues are easier to resolve relative to others, and parties weigh the significance of issues differently. In order to balance the negotiations, the 'single-undertaking' approach has been used to conclude negotiations. Single-undertaking means "there is no agreement until there is agreement on everything." Under the single-undertaking approach, all the negotiating issues are assembled into a single package. If and only if the parties feel are satisfied with the full contents of the package, then they will declare that the agreement is reached.

This agenda-setting stage of the negotiations is sometimes called "pre-negotiations." Calling the agenda-setting by the term pre-negotiations risks losing important insight into the negotiations, because parties take the agenda-setting seriously. The fact that a particular issue is on the agenda implies that no agreement is likely if there is no agreement on the issue, in the light of the single-undertaking approach. For this reason, parties strive to put their concerns and interests on the negotiating agenda.

An example may serve to highlight the significance of the agenda-setting negotiations. At the Uruguay Round, agenda-setting was an uphill battle among the advanced economies and the developing economies. The advanced economies wanted to put the issue of trade in services on the negotiating agenda, and the developing economies were strongly against the idea. On the other hand, the developing countries wanted to eliminate the farm subsidies of the advanced economies and to bring the trade barriers of the advanced economies in the textile and clothing industries into the multilateral trading regime. Through hard negotiations, the parties to the GATT agreed to negotiate all these issues under the negotiating principle of the single-undertaking.

The agenda-setting itself already opens serious negotiations. Once the WTO was established in 1995, its members worked hard to launch the first multilateral trade negotiations under the WTO. As history witnessed so well, the agenda-setting negotiations were a painful process. In November 1999, the WTO Ministerial Conference was held in Seattle. For some years, the WTO members negotiated the agenda for the new trade round, but despite hard work around the clock, the draft agenda prior to the Seattle Conference was the subject of much disagreement. It was hoped that trade ministers at Seattle would be able to compromise and launch the first trade round under the WTO. However, the disparities in the positions of the advanced economies and the developing ones proved too wide to bridge. After the demise of the much-heralded Seattle Conference, the WTO members had to work for another two years to come to agreement on the agenda for the new trade round in November 2001 at Doha, Quatar.

The issue of official language at the international negotiations is noteworthy. At international negotiations among different-language-speaking entities, parties need to clarify which language will be used at the negotiations and in the final agreement. In most business negotiations between multinational companies, practicality prevails and it is easy to adopt English, *lingua franca*, as the official language for the negotiations. However, the situation is rather different in international negotiations among sovereign nations.

At negotiations among intergovernmental organizations, different organizations adopt different official language rules. For instance, the United Nations uses English, French, Spanish, Chinese, Russian and Arabic as the official languages, meaning that all those languages are used at the United Nations meetings. At the World Trade Organization, English, French, and Spanish are recognized as the official languages. At formal meetings of the WTO, any of those three languages will be used and translated into all the other official languages. At informal meetings of the WTO, however, only English is spoken and no translation is offered. At most bilateral government-to-government negotiations, the tradition is that they negotiate in English and draft the agreement in English. This is subject to the negotiations at the agenda-setting, and parties may have compelling reasons to deviate from this tradition.

### *5.2.2 Actual negotiations*

Once the agenda is agreed, parties are set for the face-to-face talks to get the most from the negotiations. These negotiations have their own life-cycles. For talks to begin a negotiation framework is usually needed. Negotiating issues are now on the table, and parties need to move forward. For this purpose, written submission is instrumental.

Recall the case of the definition of trade in services at the Uruguay Round. At the Uruguay Round services negotiations, all the major trading nations submitted their written contributions to the negotiations. Once submitted, the documents serve as terms of reference. Of course, a party may contribute to the framework of the negotiations through talks. However, oral contribution is considered to be supplementary to the written contribution, when it comes to the framework negotiations.

A written submission is also quite significant in the bilateral negotiations; perhaps more important than in the multilateral negotiations. At the multilateral negotiations, it is usually the case that several countries submit their written submissions to the negotiations, hence there is no risk of relying on a single document for setting the negotiating framework. In trade negotiations, the U.S. and the E.U. never fail to submit their written contributions. At bilateral talks, if only one party submits the document for the negotiating framework and the other party does not do so, it is clear who gets the negotiating advantage.

Once the negotiating framework is agreed, parties move to the next stage of the negotiations: advocacy. Negotiators strive to convey to their counterparts what issues are important to them. They resort to words, documents, and actions. Formal and informal meetings are used. For some negotiating issues, negotiators present their arguments in written documents with data or legal details. When the negotiations are not progressing as they wish, they may boycott a meeting or storm out of a meeting to show their frustration. A formal meeting is the meeting among the delegations, with minutes being recorded by both sides. An informal meeting is held outside the regular formal meetings, usually among senior negotiators from both sides, when negotiators find it necessary to talk off the record.

International negotiations go through a series of rounds. During the initial rounds of talks, each side is busy advocating what it wants from the negotiations. When the negotiations move into the middle stage, negotiators try to figure out what issues are substantive and what issues are of secondary significance. At this phase of negotiations, active listening becomes important. As explained in the previous chapter, the role of the negotiator as coordinator now comes into play. Through rounds of contact, negotiators from each side get a clearer idea about the other side's win-set. With the clock ticking towards the deadline, it is essential for the negotiations to move forward that negotiators have a correct assessment of the range of possible agreements.

As the deadline approaches, negotiators are pressed to finds ways to conclude the negotiations. Considering that all the international negotiations are concluded with a written agreement, negotiators need to develop the draft text for the agreement. The draft text is a document containing items for the final agreement. Since a draft text reflects what has been negotiated up to that point of drafting, it is not a finished product, but an evolutionary product. One may liken the draft text to the framework of a building and the final text to the building itself.

The very purpose of creating the draft text is to help negotiators move forward. The drafting method is for all the agreed items and expressions to be written in a clean form of text, while those items and expressions still under negotiation are put inside brackets. At bilateral negotiations, the draft text is prepared as a joint endeavor. On the other hand, at multilateral international negotiations, it is usually the chair of the meeting who prepares the draft text.

It is important to bear in mind that the draft text is a negotiating document. This means that the timing of creating the draft text is subject to the negotiations. When is the best time to start creating the draft text? Once the draft text is produced, it is not easy to change the framework of the agreement. This inflexibility in undoing the draft text is all the more the case in multilateral negotiations. Negotiators race against time. With the deadline approaching, there is a sense of urgency to create the draft text. An attempt to prepare the draft text is going to be resisted if there is no consensus among the parties about the framework of the agreement: putting most items in brackets is not the way to go.

At international trade negotiations on market opening, negotiations proceed by the method of offer and request. Take an example of tariff negotiations: At first, countries submit their plans for reducing tariffs on products ("offer"). Upon receiving the other country's tariff reduction plan, countries request from their counterparts information about which tariffs need to be further reduced. Now, both offers and requests are on the table. Negotiators work to reduce the gaps between these offers and requests.

### *5.2.3 Deal-making*

With the deadline around the corner, negotiators are pressed to consider how to conclude the negotiations. Getting to a "done deal" requires that the agreement is within the win-set of each party. However, this requirement is only a necessary condition, not sufficient for conclusion. At the negotiations, negotiators try to get the most from the negotiations. For this purpose, they work hard to increase the size of the pie from the negotiations, and to get the largest possible slice of the pie. Negotiators cooperate to make the size of the pie as big as possible, but they compete to get the largest slice. In order to enlarge the size of the pie, negotiators may trade with each other. In the parlance of negotiations, negotiators "give and take" in order to craft a mutually beneficial deal.

The history of international negotiations is filled with cases where negotiators have failed to conclude the negotiations by the agreed deadline: the deadline has arrived, but there are still brackets in the draft text. The usual response to this stalemate is either postponement or suspension of the negotiations. Postponing negotiations means to renew the deadline and give the negotiators another chance to bridge the gaps. Suspension of the negotiations is to stop the negotiations without any scheduling of a future round of talks.

While the negotiations are suspended, negotiators and political leaders try to find a way to resurrect the negotiations. If somehow they find the way to revive talks, then negotiations can be resumed. In some cases, there is no clear-cut distinction between postponement and suspension. For instance, the Six-Party Talks on the North Korea nuclear issue has not taken place since the issuance of a joint statement in September 2005. There was no official announcement of postponement or suspension of the talks.

Sometimes, an official announcement is made. The Uruguay Round failed to conclude the agreement by December 1990. After collapse of the talks in Brussels in 1990, the Round was officially delayed to the end of 1991. The Round was still going nowhere by the end of 1991. Before the Uruguay Round was completed on December 15, 1993, the deadline was renewed three times. On the other hand, the first trade round under the WTO (known as the Doha Round) is not progressing well. It has already missed the initial deadline of 2005. The farm subsidies issue is the deal-breaker, and it shows no progress to date. As the negotiating environment was getting worse, WTO Direct General Pascal Lamy announced the suspension of the Doha Round in July 2006.

Technically speaking, making a deal requires that all the brackets in the draft text be eliminated. If there is agreement, only a single clean text remains. No matter how much negotiators talk and agree verbally, what is legally valid is what is written in the final agreed text. Hence, the drafting of the final agreement is a precise legal exercise.

The issue of language becomes important in the final text. In disputes after the agreement is in force, parties to the agreement will rely on the final text of the agreement to identify who is violation and for what. In reality, most international agreements are written in English. In non-English-speaking societies, people rely on the translated version of the agreement in the process of implementing the agreement. When disputes occur, the legal validity of the non-English version becomes problematic. Parties may avoid this problem by negotiating, and specifying, which version is authentic. Tradition has it that in cases of conflict, the English version is the authentic one.

In the Korea-China negotiations in 2000 for resolving conflicts over Chinese garlic imports to Korea, both countries drafted an agreement in both Korean and Chinese. At the Korea-U.S. FTA talks (that began in 2006), the Korean government required that the final agreement be written in English and Korean, and that both versions constitute the authentic agreement.

### *5.2.4 Ratification*

Agreement between international negotiators representing the parties is not the end of negotiations. Agreement on the final text of the agreement between negotiators signals the beginning of another process in international negotiations: ratification. An international agreement becomes effective only after the agreement is approved domestically. In most countries where representative democracy is practiced, it is the parliament or legislature which decides on ratification. Once the agreement is made internationally, the ball is in the court of the parties' domestic politics.

As history has witnessed, domestic ratification is a whole new ballgame. Agreement among negotiators is one thing, and ratification by politicians is another. Politicians are motivated by their desire to remain in power; members of parliament never forget the problem of being elected. Their actions are governed by personal incentives and political issues relating to election. On the other hand, in many cases, the negotiator is not an elected officer but a professional diplomat or a career government official whose job tenure does not coincide with the tenure of the ruling party.

At the ratification of the Free Trade Agreement with Chile, the behavior of the Korean lawmakers at the National Assembly was completely predictable, based on this set of incentives. Lawmakers from the rural districts filibustered and physically blocked the voting, resulting in the delay of the ratification process. Due to this opposition, the ratification of the agreement in Korea was as tough as the negotiations with Chile. The National Assembly had to convene four plenary meetings before lawmakers cast their votes on the agreement.

In the meantime, Korean products in Chile were deprived of any preferential trading benefits due to lack of ratification. In the process of ratification, a hefty compensation package to farmers was negotiated among the government and the politicians. Acutely aware of the upcoming election a few months down on the road, the politicians used every moment of the process of the ratification to impress their constituencies. (Choi and Lee, 2005).

Some international agreements fail ever to become effective, because major parties to the agreement fail to ratify the agreement. In this regard, the history of the ITO (International Trade Organization) is a classic example. At the Bretton Woods Conference in 1944, it was agreed to create the ITO along with the World Bank and the International Monetary Fund, all with the aim of establishing a stable international economic regime. International negotiations to create the ITO were held during 1945-1948, and the ITO charter was agreed at the Havana Conference in 1948.

However, the ITO never came into being. The principal reason for this was the failure of the U.S. to ratify the ITO charter. In 1948, U.S. elections returned a Congress that was Republican dominated, while the presidency remained in Democratic hands. By the end of 1950, President Truman announced that he would no longer seek congressional approval for the ITO. Although other countries could have gone ahead without the U.S., at this time the U.S. had emerged as the preeminent economic power in the world. No country desired to enter an ITO that did not include the U.S. (Jackson, 1997)

Why might an agreement fail to receive domestic ratification? As explained, negotiators are keenly aware of the win-set. As long as they negotiate within the boundary of the win-set, domestic failure to ratify the agreement will not happen. Does domestic failure to get political approval after international agreement imply that the theory of the win-set is flawed? The answer is no. We need to be reminded that the win-set is not fixed, but evolves over the time. As noted in the analysis of the win-set, the win-set may shift with a change of domestic political coalition through elections. In the case of ITO ratification in the U.S. in 1948-1950, the election gave rise to a new political coalition, thereby changing the win-set.

### *5.2.5 Implementation*

After ratification on the agreement is accomplished by the parties to the negotiations, now the agreement is set for the implementation. Implementation is the final destination of negotiations. Dispute is unavoidable at the phase of implementation. Dispute occurs when a party to the agreement does not enforce the agreement. In some cases, it is obvious to the parties which party is in the violation of the agreement and for what reason. In this case, remedy for the violation is rather straightforward. However, in some cases, whether a party is in violation of the agreement or not is in dispute. In these cases, resolution of the dispute may necessitate another round of negotiations.

## 5.3 Dispute Settlement Mechanisms

In the light of possible disputes during the course of implementation, parties to the negotiations may want to negotiate a dispute resolution mechanism as an integral part of the agreement. As for dispute settlement mechanisms, it is interesting to observe that there is a remarkable difference between international trade negotiations and non-trade negotiations. In most international trade negotiations, the negotiating parties create a rather elaborate system of dispute resolution, whereas no such specific dispute resolution mechanism is sought at other international negotiations.

The dispute settlement mechanism at the multilateral trading regime offers a rule-based procedure with specific regulations at each phase of dispute resolution. The rule-based dispute resolution mechanism dates back to the GATT. Negotiators at the Uruguay Round corrected some flaws of the GATT dispute settlement procedures and adopted a more specific and articulate rule, which has been incorporated as a part of the WTO. All the members of the WTO become automatically the members of the DSB (Dispute Settlement Body). The DSB governs the dispute settlement procedure, pursuant to the WTO agreement on Dispute Settlement (the full name of the agreement is 'Understanding on Rules and Procedures Governing the Settlement of Disputes'). The details of the WTO dispute settlement procedure are illustrated in <Figure 2>.

**<Figure 5.2> WTO Dispute Settlement Procedure**

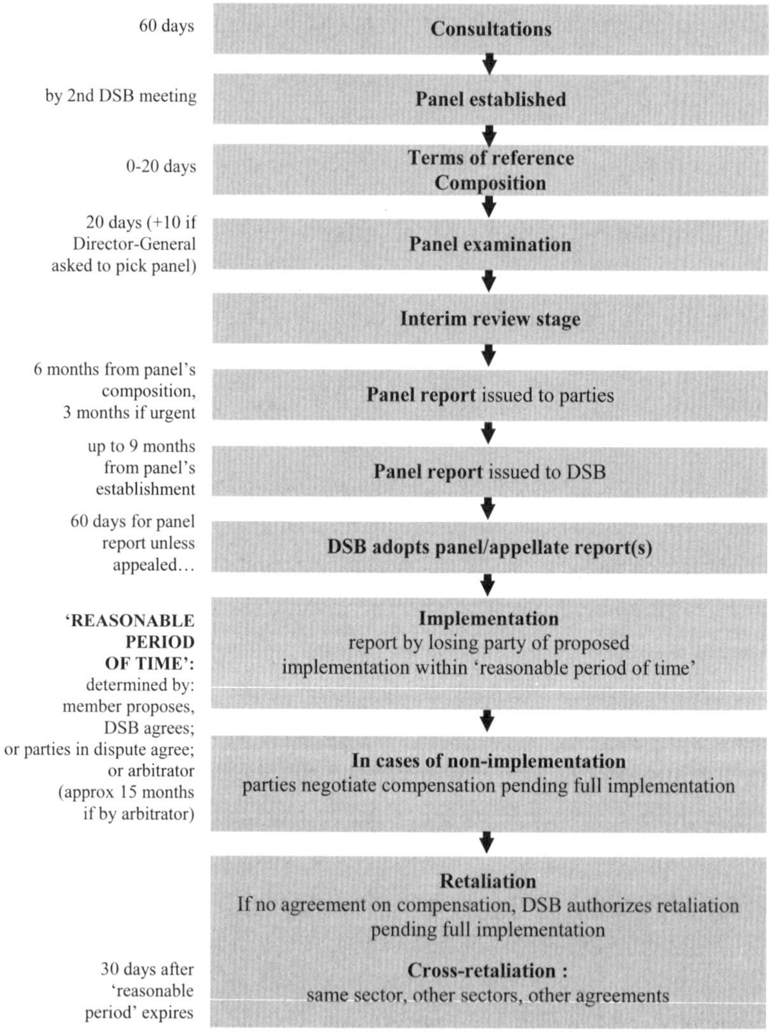


Source: WTO

Under the dispute settlement mechanism at the WTO, any member may bring to the WTO its complaint of another member's failure to enforce the WTO agreement. If the parties cannot resolve the dispute through consultation, good offices or mediation by the WTO Director General, the complaining party may request to establish a panel.

The panel is usually comprised of three trade experts from third countries not involved in the dispute. Panelists serve in their individual capacities and may not be subjected to government instructions. The panel investigates the legal validity of the complaint through written submissions and through hearings involving the parties in dispute. The panel goes through the following stages: presentation of facts and arguments from the parties to the dispute; meeting with the parties and third countries, and rebuttals; additional meetings and submissions, if required; preparation of a report on the facts and the arguments presented; submission of a factual interim report to the parties; drafting of conclusions and recommendations; and submission of the final report to the parties and the DSB. The panel is required to produce its report within the time frame of six months from the composition of the panel.

The DSB adopts the panel report unless all members of the DSB are against it. That is, if a majority of the members at the DSB are against the panel report and only the minority is for the panel report, the panel report is nevertheless adopted. This rather peculiar way of adopting a panel report at the DSB is termed the 'negative consensus.' The panel report must in principle be adopted by the DSB within 60 days. A party may appeal if it does not agree with an issue of law or the legal interpretation of the panel. A standing Appellate Body, composed of seven persons with tenure, deals with appeals. In principle, appeal proceedings should not exceed 60 days and must be completed within 90 days. The DSB adopts the Appellate Body report through the negative consensus.

If the complaining party wins its case through the DSB dispute settlement procedure, the losing party is required to bring its measure, found to be in violation of the WTO agreement, into conformity with the WTO agreement. Timing for compliance is essential. The losing party is expected to implement the DSB decision within a reasonable period of time. Usually, 18 months is the period given for implementation. In case of no satisfactory implementation, the complaining party may request authorization from the DSB to suspend trade benefits or obligations against the offending country ("retaliation").

In a FTA (Free Trade Agreement), the aims are to eliminate all tariffs on goods, and liberalize restrictions on trade in services and investment. In FTAs, it has become customary to adopt a dispute settlement procure called as 'Investor-to-State Dispute Settlement Procedure'(ISD). Under the ISD, an investor may bring its complaint about the host government to an international institution such as ICSID (International Center for Settlement of Investment Disputes) or UNCITRAL (United Nations Commission on International Trade Law). Unlike typical international dispute resolutions, where only a government may challenge other government, the ISD allows a private entity to challenge a sovereign government in a forum provided by an international organization. Hence, an investor has three venues for dealing with its complaint pursuant to an FTA: (1) arbitration at an international organization; (2) the Joint Committee of the FTA members; and (3) domestic civil court of a host government. (<Figure 3>).

Unlike these rule-based, elaborate dispute settlement mechanisms at international trade negotiations, international non-trade negotiations do not have any comparable pre-negotiated dispute resolution mechanism. Why is this the case? Members of the United Nations may bring their disputes to the International Court of Justice. However, the International Court of Justice may step in only after other parties to the dispute also consent to the jurisdiction of the Court. In the WTO or the FTA dispute settlement procedure, if a party brings its case to the dispute resolution procedure, the other party is automatically obliged to defend itself under the established dispute resolution procedure.

**<Figure 5.3> Investment-Related Dispute Settlement Procedure in FTA**

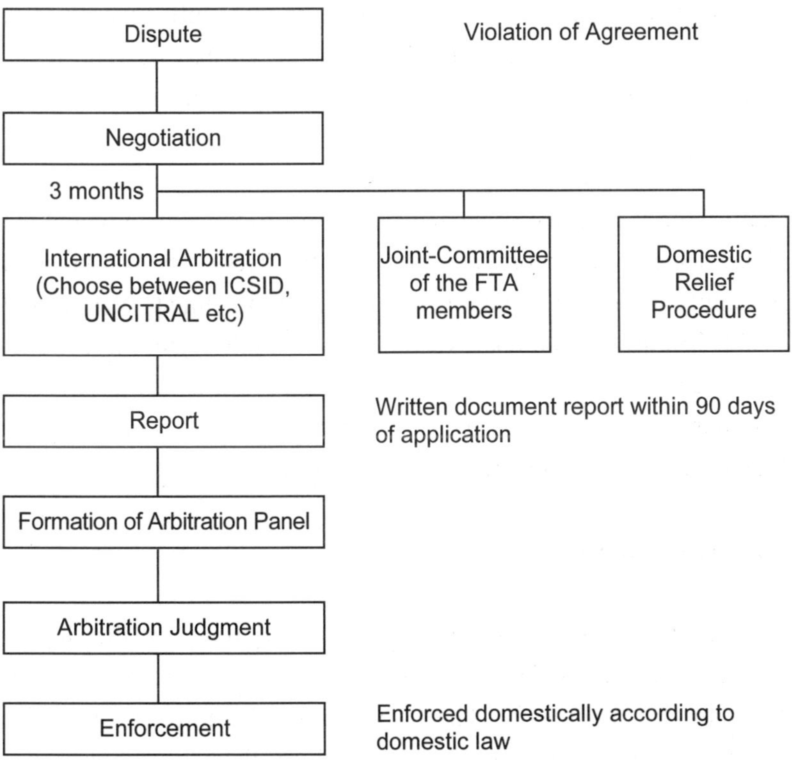

## 5.4 Case study: Climate Change Convention

### *5.4.1 From Issue to Agenda*

In the mid-1980s, there was growing public concern over global environmental issue, publicly known as the 'global warming' or 'climate change'. In particular, some island countries in the Pacific were fearful of the consequence of the global warming. They started to voice their concerns at the UN and other international organizations in order to call other countries' attention to this matter. In 1988, the World Meteorological Organization (WMO) and the UN Environment Program(UNEP) established the Intergovernmental Panel on Climate Change (IPCC), consisting of experts. The IPCC was given the mandate of making assessment report on the issue of the climate change.

In 1990, the IPCC issued its First Assessment Report. Confirming that climate change was a threat to the humanity and the global society, the report called for a global treaty. The UN General Assembly decided to launch negotiations on the climate change and established an International Negotiating Committee(INC) to conduct those negotiations. Ever since, the world has witnessed a series of multilateral negotiations under the name of the United Nations Framework Convention on Climate Change (UNFCCC).

### *5.4.2 Negotiations*

The milestone of the UNFCCC negotiations is the Kyoto Protocol. The Kyoto Protocol was negotiated and agreed in Kyoto, Japan in December 1997. The Kyoto Protocol set country specific, legally-binding targets to limit or reduce their greenhouse gas emission. It also established three innovative "mechanisms", known as joint implementation, emissions trading and clean development mechanism.

For the purpose of implementing the Kyoto Protocol, countries are separated into two general categories: developed countries, referred to as Annex 1 countries (who have accepted strict greenhouse gas emission reduction obligations); and developing countries, referred to as Non-Annex 1 countries (who have no greenhouse gas emission reduction obligations). Any Annex 1 entity failing to meet its Kyoto targets is subject to a fine and further penalised by having its reduction targets increased by 30%. By 2008, Annex 1 countries have to reduce their GHG emissions to around 5% below their 1990 levels (for many countries such as the EU members that corresponds to some 15% below their expected greenhouse gas emissions in 2008).

Negotiators came up with an interesting idea of 'emission trading.' Under this emission trading scheme, Annex 1 economies may meet their greenhouse gas targets by purchasing greenhouse gas emission reductions from elsewhere. These can be bought either from financial exchanges (such as the new EU Emissions Trading Scheme) or directly from Non-Annex 1 economies on a private basis. The emission trading scheme is in place for two main reasons. First, the cost of complying with the Kyoto Protocol is prohibitive for many Annex 1 countries (especially those countries, such as Japan or the Netherlands for example, with highly efficient, low greenhouse gas polluting industries, and high prevailing environmental standards). The Kyoto Protocol therefore allows these countries to purchase carbon credits instead of reducing greenhouse gas emissions domestically. Second, through the emission trading, Non-Annex 1 developing economies may be encouraged to reduce greenhouse gas emissions, since they can generate revenue through the sale of carbon credits.

All the Annex 1 economies have established Designated National Authorities to manage their greenhouse gas portfolios under the Kyoto Protocol. Countries including Japan, Canada, Italy, the Netherlands, Germany, France, Spain and many more, are actively promoting government carbon funds and supporting multilateral carbon funds intent on purchasing carbon credits from Non-Annex 1 countries. These government organisations are working closely with their major utility, energy, oil and gas and chemicals conglomerates to try to acquire as many greenhouse gas certificates as cheaply as possible. Virtually all of the Non-Annex 1 countries have also set up their own Designated National Authorities to manage the Kyoto process (and specifically the "clean development mechanism process" whereby these host government entities decide which greenhouse gas projects they do or do not wish to support for accreditation by the clean development mechanism executive board).

### *5.4.3 Ratification*

The Kyto Protocol met hostile domestic response in the US, the largest polluting nation now. The US Congress had already made it clear that it would not ratify any climate change convention withoug China, the potentially largest polluter in the future. Being aware of this concern, negotiators at Kyto created the conditions for enabling the Kyoto Protocol to be legally effective. They agreed that the Kyto Protocol enters into force "on the ninetieth day after the date on which not less than 55 Parties to the Convention, incorporating Parties included in Annex I which accounted in total for at least 55% of the total carbon dioxide emissions for 1990 of the Parties included in Annex I, have deposited their instruments of ratification, acceptance, approval or accession." Of the two conditions, the condition of "55 parties" was met on May 23, 2002 when Iceland ratified. The ratification by Russia on November 18, 2004 satisfied the "55%" condition and brought the treaty into force, effective February 16, 2005.

As of April 2006, a total of 163 countries have ratified the agreement (representing over 61.6% of emissions from Annex I countries). Notable exceptions include the United States and Australia. As Non-Annex 1 countries, India and China, which are not required to reduce carbon emissions, nor given any numerical target for the reduction, have ratified the protocol.

On July 25, 1997, before the Kyoto Protocol was finalized, the U.S. Senate unanimously passed by a 95–0 vote the Byrd-Hagel Resolution, which stated the sense of the Senate was that the United States should not be a signatory to any protocol that did not include binding targets and timetables for developing as well as industrialized nations or "would result in serious harm to the economy of the United States". On November 12, 1998, Vice President Al Gore symbolically signed the protocol. Both Gore and Senator Joseph Lieberman indicated that the protocol would not be acted upon in the Senate until there was participation by the developing nations. The Clinton Administration never submitted the protocol to the Senate for ratification.

The Clinton Administration released an economic analysis in July 1998, prepared by the Council of Economic Advisors, which concluded that with emissions trading and participation of key developing countries in the "Clean Development Mechanism", the costs of implementing the Kyoto Protocol could be reduced as much as 60% from many estimates. Other economic analyses, however, prepared by the Congressional Budget Office and the Department of Energy Information Administration (EIA), and others, demonstrated a potentially large decline in GDP from implementing the Protocol.

The next President, George W. Bush, has indicated that he does not intend to submit the treaty for ratification, not because he does not support the general idea, but because of the strain he believes the treaty would put on the economy. Furthermore, he made it known to the public that he was not happy with the details of the treaty. For example, he does not support the split between Annex I countries and others. Bush said of the treaty: “This is a challenge that requires a 100% effort; ours, and the rest of the world’s. The world’s second-largest emitter of greenhouse gases is China. Yet, China was entirely exempted from the requirements of the Kyoto Protocol. India and Germany are among the top emitters. Yet, India was also exempt from Kyoto … America’s unwillingness to embrace a flawed treaty should not be read by our friends and allies as any abdication of responsibility.”

Australia is another interesting case. Despite the fact that Australia was at the time of the negotiation already one of the biggest emitters on per capita basis, the country was granted an easy target of 8% increase. Nonetheless, the Australian Prime Minister, John Howard, has refused to sign the Agreement and has argued that the protocol would cost Australians jobs, and that Australia is already doing enough to cut emissions. As of 2005, Australia was the world's largest emitter per capita of greenhouse gases.

While Australia and the United States did not ratify the Kyoto Protocol, they are exploring alternative through which the climate change may be address in a collective manner: both countries signed the Asia Pacific Partnership on Clean Development and Climate at the ASEAN regional forum on 28 July 2005.

## References

Byung-il Choi and Kong-Jin Lee. 2005. 'A Long and Winding Road: Ratification of Korea's First FTA' in *Korea and International Conflicts: Case Studies,* Volume 1, edited by Byung-il Choi, Institute for International Trade and Cooperation.

Jackson, John H. 1997, *The World Trading System: Law and Policy of International Economic Relations,* second edition, the MIT Press.

*The WTO Agreement on the Dispute Settlement*, 1995.

# Chapter 6 International Negotiations Strategy

## 6.1 Introduction

This chapter wraps up our introduction to the theory and practice of international negotiation by exploring the world of international negotiations strategy. First, it will introduce a basic framework for analyzing international negotiations. The concept of efficiency of negotiation, BATNA (best alternative to negotiated agreement), interests, options and criteria will be introduced. Discussion will center on the primary questions of negotiations: when to agree and when to disagree on the draft text on the table; and how to create the maximum joint gain at the negotiations. In light of the importance of a final agreement, the effective way to draft a final agreement will be discussed.

Second, this chapter will explore the practical complexities of multilateral international negotiations in terms of process management. All the process management from agenda-setting to deal-making at the multilateral negotiations will be explained. A unique aspect of multilateral negotiations is to build coalitions among like-minded parties. The idea of coalition-building and its practical use also are discussed.

## 6.2 Framework

A layman's view of international negotiations envisions the parties either sitting across the table or shaking hands after the meeting. Imagine a United Nations Security Council Meeting. What brings those people to the table? What happens if they cannot reach an expected outcome of the meeting? Will there be any future round of talks? What if the next round of talks would be unsatisfactory? How will they know whether to agree or disagree on the draft proposal on the table?

Representatives come to the negotiating table because the principals have conflicts on issues. When the member nations of the UN Security Council convene for a meeting, the meeting is a concrete act of choice: they have chosen to engage in negotiations instead of resorting to other means, such as war. Negotiations take place since people want to resolve their conflicts in a peaceful manner. This basic fact is important to bear in mind. The recognition that the negotiation itself is the product of deliberate choice on both sides of the table leads to recognition of another important basic fact: that a party to the negotiations has choices other than negotiations. These other choices available to the negotiator are called 'alternatives.' The fact that the parties came to the negotiating table implies that each side places some hope in the outcome of the negotiations, despite of her alternatives outside of the negotiations.

In case there is no agreement at the end of negotiations, each side to the negotiations will consider these alternatives. Conceptually, each side can figure out which is the best among these alternatives. The best alternative a negotiator can pursue in the case of disagreement is called the BATNA (Best Alternative To a Negotiated Agreement) (Fisher and Ury 1981). Through negotiations, each side tries to achieve an outcome superior to her BATNA.

How does a party achieve a negotiating outcome better than the BATNA? Since the negotiations are a mutual endeavor where each side is at odds with the other side, an effort to wrest the larger slice of the pie from the other is not going to be easy. Hence, the necessity for cooperation between both sides to the negotiations looms large.

Every negotiation has two aspects: cooperation and competition among the negotiators. Negotiators cooperate in order to create the largest possible joint gain from the negotiations. They compete in order to get the largest share of the joint gain. As an analogy, first they cooperate to enlarge the size of the pie, and later they compete to get the largest slice of the pie.

Suppose party A and party B can create joint value V from the negotiations. Denoting the share of party A from the negotiations S(A), and the share of party B from the negotiations S(B), it must be the case that

$$S(A) + S(B) \leq V$$

Each of party A and party B cooperate in order to maximize V and compete to maximize its own share S(A) and S(B). In case of disagreement, party A gets its BATNA, denoted as D(A), and party B gets its BATNA, denoted as D(B). Any agreement should satisfy the condition of individual rationality as follows:

$$S(A) \geq D(A)$$
$$S(B) \geq D(B)$$

**<Figure 6.1> Gains from the Negotiations**

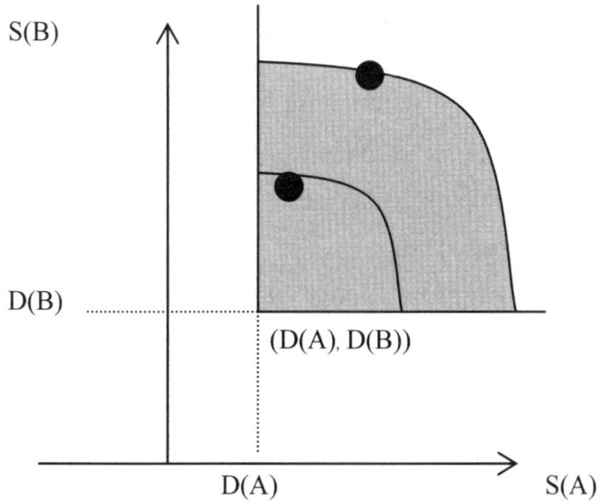


In <Figure 1>, the shaded area illustrates a possible gain from the negotiations. The two points within the shaded area illustrate possible agreement. However, the point located inside the shaded area is inefficient compared with another point located along the frontier of the shaded area. An agreement point located to the south-west of the frontier can be improved, because each party to the negotiations can claim a larger share without decreasing the share of other party If at a particular agreement a party can find another agreement where she can improve her share without decreasing the other party's share, the existing agreement is said to be "inefficient."

At the frontier of the shaded area, no such joint improvement of the share is possible. Thus, we see that any agreement along the frontier of the shaded area is efficient. In order to get the maximum possible share from the negotiations, negotiators should be able to agree on a point along the frontier of the shaded area. Agreeing to a point inside of the frontier gives rise to an inefficient outcome, meaning that negotiators leave joint gains on the table.

Unfortunately, gains from the negotiations are hard to quantify at many international negotiations. Therefore, how can we assure that a good negotiating outcome is achieved? We may claim that a negotiation is satisfactory when it achieves a sa*tisfactory* outcome through a s*atisfactory* process. What counts are process and outcome, because sovereign nations may encounter each other in other contexts in international affair.

Using the jargon of game theory, nations are at a repeated game. To achieve the best outcome in the repeated game, a long-term perspective is essential. If a country tries to take advantage of another country due to the peculiarities of a particular negotiation, it may regret its short-sightedness at a later encounter where its negotiating leverage is less than its counterpart's. This consideration leads to the conclusion that relationships matter in international negotiations. However, one should not be mistakenly led to believe that relationships should be preserved no matter what. It is the maintenance of a good working relationship, not the relationship *per se* that needs to be preserved. For instance, the U.S. regards China as a rival and a potential hegemonic power in the future. Despite this adversarial relationship, the U.S. tries to maintain a good working relationship with China.

When do we know that a good outcome is achieved, and a good process is maintained at negotiations? There are many theories which may serve as reference. Among these theories, the "seven elements" from Roger Fisher at Harvard University is one of the most commonly-cited references. Roger Fisher (1981) identified 'seven elements' for a good negotiating outcome in his book 'Getting to Yes.' Fisher's seven elements have been popularized in various negotiations. It is a consulting device and a reliable framework for negotiations in arbitration, too.

According to Fisher, an agreement is considered good, if it

fulfills the following seven conditions:

1. The agreement is better than the BATNA;
2. The agreement serves mutual INTERESTS well;
3. The agreement is among the best of many OPTIONS;
4. The agreement is based on objective and legitimate CRITERIA;
5. The agreement contains specific and operational COMMITMENTS;
6. The agreement is reached through effective COMMUNICATIONS;
7. The agreement helps to build a good working RELATIONSHIP.

The concepts of BATNA and relationship have been introduced already in the preceding paragraphs. It cannot be emphasized enough that international negotiations take place in the context of long-term relationships and through communications. The negotiating sessions themselves are the venue for communication. Without effective two-way communication, negotiators would have limited knowledge about other side's concerns, interests, and preference on the negotiating agenda.

**<Figure 6.2> The 'Seven Elements' for an Effective Negotiation**

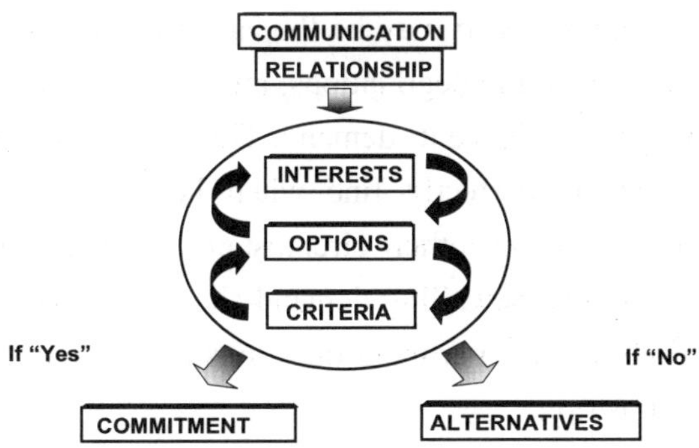


Source: Constructed on the basis of Fisher et al (1981)

In <Figure 2>, which captures the essential idea of Fisher et al (1981), the circle illustrates the value circle at negotiations. It shows that negotiators can improve their mutual gains through exploring their interests. In reality, negotiators may insist upon a particular position. For instance, in the sales negotiations of the new civil aircraft with Singapore Airlines, Airbus may stick to a particular price. Surely, it is in the interest of any seller to sell at the highest possible price to a buyer, as it is in the interest of any buyer to get the lowest possible price from the seller. For the better negotiations, a negotiator from Singapore Airlines should ask the following questions to her counterpart from Airbus:

(1) Why do you stick to this particular price?
(2) What leads you to believe the price you ask is a reasonable price?
(3) Is there any other way to meet your needs other than price?

Through these questions, the Singapore Airlines negotiator explores what lies behind the price demand of the Airbus negotiator.

As it turns out in many international business negotiations, price is only one parameter of many about which the party is concerned; the full set of these parameters constitute the final agreement. When a party is stubbornly adamant on a particular price, there must be some reason behind this. It may be the case that he believes that he has the upper hand in the negotiations, and thereby wants to make a 'take it at this price or leave it' demand. This way of making 'take-it-or-leave-it' offer is perfectly fine when he possesses monopoly power. However, under other circumstances where he is not a monopolist, such a stonewalling demand should be challenged. How? As explained above, ask pertinent questions to figure out what leads him to such a position.

In the above example, the Singapore Airlines negotiator tries to clarify the interests behind the positions. Quite often, the Airbus negotiator may not respond to question (1). Then, the Singapore Airlines negotiator goes on to ask questions (2) and (3). Question (2) is about criteria, and (3) is about options. By alternating these questions back and forth, the Singapore Airlines negotiator may have a better grasp of the unspoken interests of her counterpart. This is precisely what happens at most international negotiations. In order to fathom the hidden interests of other side, one needs to be persistent and creative in asking questions. Direct questions about unspoken and hidden interests and indirect questions via criteria and options all prove useful.

For one reason or another, at the outset of the negotiations some negotiators simply declare what they want from the negotiations, and adhere to this position. This style of negotiation may lead the negotiator's counterpart to respond in kind. Suppose his counterpart commits to a similar tactic and sticks to a particular negotiating stance ("positioning"). Then, two positions, which are likely quite distant from each other, will be set. If this is the case, the negotiating process becomes a tug of war. It is likely that these negotiations will end up with an agreement on the mid-point.

Unfortunately, there is also a high chance that such an outcome is an inefficient outcome. This is because these negotiators never bothered to think beyond their tug-of-war test of toughness; they failed to explore any common grounds for resolving their conflict. All they did was to compete for gain at the expense of the other side, and there was no cooperation to increase mutual gain. Mindless persistence may give rise to a sorry result where mutual gains are left on the negotiating table. Mutual gains should have been created and claimed in the course of a more productive negotiating process.

For an instance, if elder sister wants the peel of orange for baking and younger sister wants the fruit of orange for eating, then cutting the orange in half is not the best possible option. In realities such inefficient outcome does happen time and again, because people at the negotiations do not seriously ask their counterpart's genuine interest. They presume that they know their counterpart's interest, which may turn out to be position, not interest. This sort of positional negotiations is indication that people do not have effective two-way communication.

Criteria refer to principle, standard, or practice, which is used to evaluate options. At the negotiations, many options are created and explored. If there is to be agreement, negotiators should opt for some options. How will they agree on particular options? Criteria will guide this decision-making. Precedent, scientific truth, established business practice, international law, and internationally accepted standard are examples of criteria. Since negotiators use criteria to evaluate options at the bargaining table, criteria should be fair and objective.

For this purpose, the method of "I cut and you choose" Is a commonly adopted technique at international negotiations. This is a cake-cutting analogy. Under this scheme, the person, who will cut the cake will try to make the division of the cake as fair as possible, since the other person will choose which slice she will get. The international negotiations on subsidy used this scheme of "I cut and you choose" to ensure the fair and impartial criteria. Details of these negotiations are discussed in the next section.

If the negotiations are successful, there will be commitment. Commitment is a mutually agreed promise to do something pursuant to the agreed-upon time frame. At international negotiations, commitment is almost always recorded in a written document, named as the final agreement. The importance of the written agreement at international negotiations cannot be emphasized enough. At the end of long and tough negotiations, what remains after negotiators leave the negotiations table is a written document named the final agreement. This final agreement is important for two reasons: first, for the domestic ratification, and second, for the implementation.

First, the final agreement signed by negotiators cannot be effective, unless it gets ratification. In a democratic country, this ratification is done at the parliament (the National Assembly in Korea, and the Congress in the US and so on) whose members are elected through popular vote. In other country where people are not represented by the parliament, domestic authoritarian dictator will decide whether to approve the agreement or not.

In case of bilateral agreement, the agreement becomes effective if and only if both countries ratify it. On the other hand, the case of multilateral agreement is a bit different. As we have seen in the case of the Kyoto Protocol in the previous chapter, participants to the multilateral negotiations usually set a threshold of the necessary number of countries, which ratify the agreement. If this threshold is reached, the multilateral agreement becomes effective.

If the final agreement becomes effective, then the implementation stage kicks in. Common observation of the implementation of international agreement is that countries more often than not dispute each other. Quite often, these disputes arise due to the incomplete nature of the final agreement, because negotiators cannot completely foresee the future events. While the inescapable incompleteness of foresight gives rise to the inevitable incomplete agreement, some disputes arise due to countries' different interpretation of the agreement.

In this light, the final agreement should be as specific as possible, should set an unambiguous standard for implementation, consequently leaving less room for the dispute during the implementation stage. Henceforth, the agreement should be drafted along the measurable indicators. These indicators, based on the mutual agreement, should be achievable and realistic for the parties to the negotiations. In short, the drafting of the final agreement should abide by the guideline of SMART (Specific, Measurable, Achievable, Realistic, and Time-frame).

## 6.3 Mutilateral International Negotiations

A common aspect of international negotiations is that they are conducted among many governments. This n-party negotiation process is called multilateral negotiation. The multilateral negotiation poses different challenges to, and opportunities for negotiators compared with bilateral negotiations between only two parties. Imagine the UN, where about 200 governments participate in the negotiations. About 150 governments (or technically economies) negotiate at the WTO. Considering the vastly divergent interests among these governments, it would be difficult, if not impossible, to proceed without order.

To have a multilateral negotiation, there are many organizational details to be taken care of: agenda, document distribution, recording the meeting, and so on. Without orderly process management, multilateral negotiations will become chaotic. The response to many of the logistical challenges is coordinated by the secretariat of an international organization, which sponsors the multilateral negotiations. For instance, the UN offers the venue for the negotiation, and the UN staffs facilitate the meeting through document distribution, and simultaneous interpretation.

At multilateral international negotiations, there is an established protocol of process management. To facilitate proceedings, at every meeting there is a chair. The Chair is usually selected by the participants. The Chair presides over the meeting: she calls the meeting, introduces the agenda, and opens the floor for discussion. Up to this point, it is all rather mechanical.

However, at multilateral international negotiations, many different views are likely to be presented. As the negotiations proceed over the time, negotiators try to narrow their differences. Despite hard work and effort by the participants, this is a difficult task. Here, the Chair plays a key role. She is expected to draw up and present a draft proposal which reflects the negotiations, summarizes contending views, assesses differences among views, and proposes a way forward. This role of chair is that of a facilitator; a key role.

The Chair does not make such a draft proposal unless there is a consensus among negotiators to ask her to prepare it, and the issue of timing becomes critical. An early draft proposal may hinder further exploration for interests and options. Depending on the complexity of negotiations, it may take a long time to realise a draft proposal by the Chair.

Decision-making at multilateral negotiations is the next key issue. What is the best way to make decision? There is no a single answer to this. Different international organizations have established different decision-making rules. For instance, no proposal is approved at the UN Security Council if any Permanent Member is against it ('veto'). The UN general assembly uses majority voting. On the other hand, the WTO uses consensus as a decision-making rule. Consensus is a situation where no one is against the proposal on the table. There is a subtle distinction between unanimity and consensus. Unanimity is a situation where a roll call is conducted and each and everyone present expressed her affirmative position to the proposal. In judging whether consensus is achieved or not, usually no such a roll call is done. A common practice at international negotiations is to open the floor for discussion on the proposal and to check whether there is any outspoken objection to the proposal.

Coalition-building is a unique aspect of multilateral negotiations. A coalition is a group of countries which share the same interest on a particular issue. Quite often these coalitions are called groups of like-minded countries. Sometimes they they refer to themselves as a "friends" group. Whatever the expression, the purpose of coalition-making is the same: to represent their common interests at multilateral negotiations more strongly.

There are some well-known coalitions at international negotiations such as the Cairns Group and the G-77. The Cairns Group was formed among agriculture exporting countries, pressing for more open and freer trade in farm products. The members of the Cairns Groups complain that, unlike trade in merchandise, trade in agriculture faces high tariffs and various other import restrictions. At international trade negotiations, on the issue of agricultural trade, they unite behind a common negotiating position. The G-77 is the group of self-proclaimed developing countries, formed in the mid 1960s. Based on their low income and underdeveloped economies, the G-77 speaks for specific and differential treatment for its members in international trade. In the early days of its formation, the G-77 carried some negotiating leverage as a group.

One should not be mistaken by believing that every member of these coalitions takes an identical stand on the whole negotiating agenda. Coalitions are forged on the basis of issue. It is not unusual to find two countries belonging to a coalition at odds with each other over a different issue outside of the coalition. For instance, Australia and Thailand are both members of the Cairns Group. However, Australia usually presses for more market-opening in service sector, while Thailand is usually defensive on this issue.

## 6.4 Putting Theory to Work

### *6.4.1 Case A: International Subsidy Agreement*

International trade negotiations on subsidies were sharply divided into two groups. Some argued subsidies were bad, because subsidies, financial or equivalent grants from the government to local companies or industries, distorted international trade flows by giving local companies or industries an artificial advantage. Others argued that subsidies were good, because they helped increase the competitiveness of backward industries through research and development. The former developed their logic through their attack on farm subsidies, while the latter developed their logic through their praise of R&D.

After years of negotiations, negotiators came to the agreement that subsidies would be classified into three types: prohibited, allowed, and actionable. The meaning of the prohibited subsidy and allowed subsidy is evident. The actionable subsidy is a subsidy, which a government may grant, but another government may challenge. In order to establish more legal certainty, they first negotiated the list of the prohibited subsidies and that of the allowed subsidies. However, as this list could not be exhaustive, they agreed that it was only "illustrative."

How then do we know whether a particular subsidy is allowed or not? Here, the idea of the actionable subsidy comes into play. Suppose a government gives a subsidy to its local firm, and the subsidy is not on the list of either allowed subsidies or prohibited subsidies. Then, another government may challenge the validity of such a subsidy. Instead of tackling impossible task of drawing a fine line between the allowed and the prohibited subsidy, negotiators came up with a useful option of the category of the actionable subsidy.

Once a challenge is made, a panel will decide whether the challenge stands or not, on the basis of the degree of trade distortion caused by the subsidy in the question to the complaining country. Here the degree of distortion is criteria. A panel composed of experts from third countries to the dispute will be in charge of the case. Such a panel serves as an impartial and objective criterion.

### *6.4.2 Case B: The six-party talk commitment*

On September 19, 2005, the US, China, Japan, Russia, Republic of Korea and DPRK issued the Joint Statement of the Six Party Talk in Beijing, which was launched to address DPRK's nuclear program. The following is the text of the Joint Statement.

**Joint Statement of the Fourth Round of the Six-Party Talks**

**Beijing 19 September 2005**

The Fourth Round of the Six-Party Talks was held in Beijing, China among the People's Republic of China, the Democratic People's Republic of Korea, Japan, the Republic of Korea, the Russian Federation, and the United States of America from July 26th to August 7th, and from September 13th to 19th, 2005.

Mr. Wu Dawei, Vice Minister of Foreign Affairs of the PRC, Mr. Kim Gye Gwan, Vice Minister of Foreign Affairs of the DPRK; Mr. Kenichiro Sasae, Director-General for Asian and Oceanian Affairs, Ministry of Foreign Affairs of Japan; Mr. Song Min-soon, Deputy Minister of Foreign Affairs and Trade of the ROK; Mr. Alexandr Alekseyev, Deputy Minister of Foreign Affairs of the Russian Federation; and Mr. Christopher Hill, Assistant Secretary of State for

East Asian and Pacific Affairs of the United States attended the talks as heads of their respective delegations.

Vice Foreign Minister Wu Dawei chaired the talks.

For the cause of peace and stability on the Korean Peninsula and in Northeast Asia at large, the Six Parties held, in the spirit of mutual respect and equality, serious and practical talks concerning the denuclearization of the Korean Peninsula on the basis of the common understanding of the previous three rounds of talks, and agreed, in this context, to the following:

1. The Six Parties unanimously reaffirmed that the goal of the Six-Party Talks is the verifiable denuclearization of the Korean Peninsula in a peaceful manner.

The DPRK committed to abandoning all nuclear weapons and existing nuclear programs and returning, at an early date, to the Treaty on the Non-Proliferation of Nuclear Weapons and to IAEA safeguards.

The United States affirmed that it has no nuclear weapons on the Korean Peninsula and has no intention to attack or invade the DPRK with nuclear or conventional weapons.

The ROK reaffirmed its commitment not to receive or deploy nuclear weapons in accordance with the 1992 Joint Declaration of the Denuclearization of the Korean Peninsula, while affirming that there exist no nuclear weapons within its territory.

The 1992 Joint Declaration of the Denuclearization of the Korean Peninsula should be observed and implemented.

The DPRK stated that it has the right to peaceful uses of nuclear energy. The other parties expressed their respect and agreed to discuss, at an appropriate time, the subject of the provision of light water reactor to the DPRK.

2. The Six Parties undertook, in their relations, to abide by the

purposes and principles of the Charter of the United Nations and recognized norms of international relations.

The DPRK and the United States undertook to respect each other's sovereignty, exist peacefully together, and take steps to normalize their relations subject to their respective bilateral policies.

The DPRK and Japan undertook to take steps to normalize their relations in accordance with the Pyongyang Declaration, on the basis of the settlement of unfortunate past and the outstanding issues of concern.

3. The Six Parties undertook to promote economic cooperation in the fields of energy, trade and investment, bilaterally and/or multilaterally.

China, Japan, ROK, Russia and the US stated their willingness to provide energy assistance to the DPRK.

The ROK reaffirmed its proposal of July 12th 2005 concerning the provision of 2 million kilowatts of electric power to the DPRK.

4. The Six Parties committed to joint efforts for lasting peace and stability in Northeast Asia.

The directly related parties will negotiate a permanent peace regime on the Korean Peninsula at an appropriate separate forum.

The Six Parties agreed to explore ways and means for promoting security cooperation in Northeast Asia.

5. The Six Parties agreed to take coordinated steps to implement the afore-mentioned consensus in a phased manner in line with the principle of "commitment for commitment, action for action".

6. The Six Parties agreed to hold the Fifth Round of the Six-Party Talks in Beijing in early November 2005 at a date to be determined through consultations.

This Joint Statement offers a useful text for examining the guideline of the drafting the commitment. Check this Statement against the guideline of SMART. The following four paragraphs, among others, reveal problems of drafting:

(a) The Democratic People's Republic of Korea (North Korea) committed to abandoning all nuclear weapons and existing nuclear programs and returning at an early date to the treaty on the nonproliferation of nuclear weapons (NPT) and it IAEA (International Atomic Energy Agency) safeguards.
(b) The directly related parties will negotiate a permanent peace regime on the Korean Peninsula at an appropriate separate forum.
(c) The other parties expressed their respect and agreed to discuss at an appropriate time the subject of the provision of light-water reactor to the DPRK.
(d) The six parties agreed to take coordinated steps to implement the aforementioned consensus in a phased manner in line with the principle of "commitment for commitment, action for action."

Can you identify the drafting problems? We will leave you to identify and address the problems yourself and in discussion with your colleagues and professors, as this concludes our introduction to the theory and practice of international negotiations. We hope that you find the techniques and case studies interesting and illustrative in helping you understand the complexities of contemporary international interaction.

## References

Byung-il Choi. 2005. 'A Long and Winding Road: Ratification of Korea's First FTA' in *Korea and International Conflicts: Case Studies,* Volume 1, edited by Byung-il Choi, Institute for International Trade and Cooperation.

Fisher, Roger, William Ury and Bruce Patton. 1981. *Getting to Yes: Negotiating Agreement Without Giving In.* New York: Penguin.